Escape *to* Reality

How the World is Changing **Gardening**, and **Gardening** is Changing the World

MARK CULLEN
with BEN CULLEN

NIMBUS
PUBLISHING
— NIMBUS.CA —

Nimbus Publishing Limited
3660 Strawberry Hill Street, Halifax, NS, B3K 5A9
(902) 455-4286 nimbus.ca

Printed and bound in Canada

NB1385

Editor: Paula Sarson
Cover Design: Heather Bryan
Interior Design: Jenn Embree

Library and Archives Canada Cataloguing in Publication
Cullen, Mark, 1956-, author
Escape to reality : how the world is changing gardening, and gardening is changing the world / Mark Cullen with Ben Cullen.
Includes bibliographical references and index.
Issued in print and electronic formats.
ISBN 978-1-77108-693-6 (hardcover).
—ISBN 978-1-77108-694-3 (HTML)

1. Gardening—Philosophy. 2. Gardens—Philosophy. 3. Gardening—Canada. 4. Gardens—Canada. I. Cullen, Ben, author
II. Title.

SB454.3.P45C85 2018   635.01   C2018-902882-3
C2018-902883-1

Nimbus Publishing acknowledges the financial support for its publishing activities from the Government of Canada, the Canada Council for the Arts, and from the Province of Nova Scotia. We are pleased to work in partnership with the Province of Nova Scotia to develop and promote our creative industries for the benefit of all Nova Scotians.

Dedicated to the 159 Canadian men and women who lost their lives in the Afghanistan conflict. All royalties from the sale of this book will be donated to the Highway of Heroes Living Tribute.

We are planting 117,000 trees on the Highway of Heroes, one for each of Canada's war dead since 1812, plus, 1.8 million trees on either side of the highway, one for each Canadian who volunteered for military service during times of war.
For our freedom.

Details at hohtribute.ca.

CONTENTS

❧

Part III
THE VALUE OF THE GARDENING EXPERIENCE

Part IV
SOWING A VISION

PREFACE

*I only went out for a walk and finally concluded to
stay out till sundown, for going out, I found,
was really going in.*

—John Muir (1838–1914)

A highly accomplished American journalist living in London, England, takes a walk in the park each day for some months; it changes everything. He feels better, has more energy, his memory improves (no more sticky notes on his computer screen), and he feels less stressed.

A seven-year-old child who was once "addicted" to computer games was afraid of the outdoors. He wanted to stay indoors, "where the electrical outlets are." He felt safe there. He understood it and there were no bad things to make him nervous. Once he was introduced to the outdoor experience, the same kid was able to shed the false security from four walls and a climate-controlled environment. He discovered that there was adventure out there, in wide open spaces that engaged his intellect and imagination. He was challenged in ways that he could only have imagined while indoors, and only if a computer program led him down that path. The metamorphosis experienced by this child out of doors inspired the writing of the landmark book *Last Child in the Woods* by Richard Louv, published in 2005.

I went to visit an old friend, a very "senior" senior; okay, he was ninety-seven. Hugh Beaty could only move around using a walker. He was on oxygen and was housebound in a modern facility built for the aged. To all intents and purposes, he was well taken care of. Clean, well fed, and before bed he was allowed one ounce of his favourite Scotch to help him sleep. Life was grand, except when it wasn't.

"What do you miss most, Hugh?" I asked.

"Freedom to move and go out of doors," he answered.

"How would you like to go for a drive? It is a beautiful July day and we can roll the windows down," I said.

He looked at me incredulously. It was a look that I had become used to, one that said, *Are you out of your mind?* A pregnant pause while he thought about it.

"*Yeah!* Let's do it." The words had no sooner left his mouth than he was gently tugging at the translucent tubes that flowed from a portable oxygen tank up his nostrils.

"Are you okay without your oxygen, Hugh?"

He assured me that he was just fine.

Slowly, carefully, with some assistance, we manoeuvred the big man into my car. He landed in the passenger side bucket seat with a quiet thump. I tossed his walker into my trunk and slid into the driver's seat.

"Where would you like to go?" I asked as we pulled away from the curb.

"I don't know. But this is nice," was all he said.

"How 'bout I take you to the farm?"

Another sidelong stare. "Really?"

"Why not. It is only ten minutes away. We can see how things have changed since you left a few months ago."

It was agreed. Windows down, wind gently blowing into the cabin of the car, we were off.

As I pulled slowly into the driveway, I knew there was no way that I could get him out of the car, so I pulled in to park square to the front of the house that Hugh was born in, where he had spent all but four years—the "war years" of 1940–1944. I parked directly in front of the steps that he had hidden under when he was four years old, trying to get away from a father who was about to mete out some well-deserved discipline for some infraction on Hugh's part.

"Would you like a coffee?" I asked, as I reached around to the back seat of the car for my Thermos. He accepted my offer. I poured. And we sat for a long moment, enjoying the shade of his sugar maple tree on a typical summer day.

I didn't really know how much Hugh enjoyed that trip until three weeks later, at his funeral. His son Bob told me that his dad had called him the same day at his home in Calgary to say that I had picked him up and taken him to "the farm." A trip down the road with fresh air flowing through the windows. A moment to reflect on the past.

A man discovers a new life through the discipline of walking through public parks in the densely populated UK city of London. A child discovers a world of adventure outside the four walls of his home, the only one he really knew, until he discovered a different place in his own backyard. And an elderly friend revisits his past on a final trip to his family farm.

As a lifetime gardener and writer, I am fascinated by the changes that have taken place over the last couple of generations in the Canadian garden and by nature's power to affect us. Not too many years ago, we adopted chemicals and machinery to mould and craft our landscapes into images that suited us, regardless of the environmental costs: 2,4-D and gas-powered leaf blowers are two cases in point.

We gardeners are now passionate people with less of an interest in the newest rose introduction or another addition to our dahlia collection but a much greater interest in attracting pollinators, creating biodiversity, and pursuing the social benefits of the gardening experience through community gardens, social media, and even farmers' markets.

This book explores this new mentality. It exposes the gardening experience as something that it seldom gets credit for: the original "green profession" with a pedigree that has changed and continues to change at remarkable speed. Whether you garden or not, we are all affected by gardens.

Escape to Reality turns our attention away from the things that distract us, many of them electronic, and focuses our attention on experiences and lessons from the world outside four walls, many of them in our own yards.

In this age of mindfulness, we have written this book to bring focus to the greatest auditorium the world has ever experienced, where mindfulness can be practised easily and regularly. My son Ben and I invite you to reflect with us on the journey Canadians are on, out of doors, right outside your doors. (Ben's contributions are interspersed and noted throughout the book; otherwise, the selections are mine.)

The world is changing the gardening experience. And the new gardening experience is changing the world.

—Mark and Ben Cullen

Part I

Embracing Nature

What is this life if, full of care,
We have no time to stand and stare.
—William H. Davies (1871–1940), "Leisure"

ow often do we produce a natural thought? When we think of eating or drinking. When we think of sex. When we think of going to sleep. All natural thoughts, right? How often do we think of nature? Our connection to the natural world is a subject of much discussion today, as it should be. After all, with every electronic message received and sent, every YouTube video watched, and every time we plug ear buds into our ears we disconnect ourselves from the natural world by small but measurable degrees.

We have become a society that believes in the myth that humans stand alone in the natural world, with walls between us and the wind that blows outside of our front doors—literally and figuratively. We have bought into our own advertising that we are better, faster, smarter than Nature herself.

It seems we have forgotten the work of early naturalists, such as Alexander von Humboldt, who showed us long ago that nature and humans are deeply interconnected. He was perhaps among the world's earliest environmentalists and the first to describe "climate change." Based on observations in 1802, while studying the effects of agricultural irrigation and deforestation around Lake Valencia, South America, according to Andrea Wulf, he claimed, "The action of humankind across the globe could affect future generations." He was among the first to explain the fundamental functions of the forest for the ecosystem and climate: the trees' ability to store water and to enrich the atmosphere with moisture, their protection of the soil, and their cooling effect.

According to his early writing, Humboldt described nature as a web, featuring intricately balanced interdependent organisms. "Everything," he explained, "is interaction and reciprocal." While Humboldt's thesis is now over two hundred years old, we still debate the role of nature in the human world—as if these are separate.

Part I provides a view of the gardening experience and the gardener that is new to the previous generation of gardeners, mine (I am, after all, a baby boomer). Those of us brought up with 2,4-D, malathion, and Cygon 2E at our parents' knee knew a different experience in the yard and garden. It was more controlling than it is today. This is a change worthy of celebration. Canadian gardeners now are more open-minded, slower, quieter, and better connected to the natural world.

When Ben and I speak publicly, we talk about biodiversity, the decline of the honeybee and monarch butterfly populations, benefits of planting native flowers and trees, and how the outdoor gardening experience is a good one for young and old. None of this was relevant twenty years ago.

Our escape to reality begins by embracing nature, and Canada may be the best place in the world to do it. We are blessed, after all, with a grand abundance of it.

Chapter 1
Gardening Success

Shall I not have intelligence with the earth? Am I not partly leaves and vegetable mould myself?

—Henry David Thoreau (1817–1862)

As I look in my crystal ball, I see gardens of the future that hinge on an old-fashioned concept of "feeding the soil." It is interesting to see how we have come full circle in about three generations.

Before the Second World War there were precious few chemical "solutions" available to the home gardener. Then along came a plethora of choices for weed control (2,4-D), insect control (malathion, Cygon 2E, and even DDT), and everything changed. Many professionals endorsed enthusiastically the new "remedies" for garden "problems" that had plagued them for years.

It has taken this long, since about 1945, for Canadians to realize there is a better way, a more responsible and sustainable way, to produce a great garden. It starts with compost, and it includes the elimination of many synthetic "solutions."

In fact, I argue that the greatest solution of all is the realization that there are no magic bullets. We reap what we sow, even where soil is concerned: gardening success = great soil; and great soil = gardening success. It really is that simple.

You have a dream of an amazing garden. Perhaps, in your mind's eye, you can see plants loaded with colour galore, others hanging with fruit and vegetables in abundance. You see songbirds, butterflies, and hummingbirds calling in at your place, choosing it as their home this summer.

All of us have these dreams. And in my case, these dreams are reality, though I would be the first to admit that the season never unfolds quite like I had imagined it in the dreamy, snow-filled days of winter. However, the disappointments are always balanced with good surprises: Mother Nature is like that, never predictable.

One thing that I *can* predict, though, is this: if you prepare the soil well, you are far more likely to see your gardening dreams become reality. I remind you of the farmer's number one rule: *feed the soil*. All farmers, but organic farmers especially, know that when they add nutrients to the soil amazing things happen. Seeds germinate, plants grow, and disease and insect infestations are minimized (no, they don't go away). In short, the soil is to plants what the dinner table is to humans. It is where they go to get life.

The first week of May is Compost Awareness Week in Canada. What are you doing to celebrate? Myself, I am hauling in a truckload of the good stuff and beginning my planting season in earnest by spreading it wherever I am planting.

WHY COMPOST?

Consider what compost is: decomposed natural material. Your banana peels, egg shells, and coffee grounds break down to a higher purpose. As they rot, they marry up with other organic materials, water, and oxygen, to become alive with the most precious things in life: microbes, beneficial bacteria, insects, annelids (namely, earthworms), and mycorrhiza. Indeed, without the alchemy of compost your garden would languish in an inert soup of tired medium. Roots would not thrive, and the top portion of plants would just sit there at best or die, at worst.

MY TOP FIVE SOIL ENHANCEMENT TIPS

Here is how to create a successful garden, however you define it:

1. **Spread it deep.** Last year's garden used up much of the nutrition in the soil. Now is the time to replenish it with generous quantities of finished compost. Compost from your composting unit works, but generally there is precious little of it to show for all your trekking out there with kitchen scraps. Acquire quality compost by the twenty-kilogram bag at your favourite garden retailer, and look for composted cattle or sheep manure that is certified by the Compost Quality Alliance. BioMax is the trade name, and this is the good stuff: it is safer to use than many other composts as it has been properly composted, or "cooked." Spread it three to five centimetres thick and dig it in.

2. **Earthworms.** Let the earthworms turn your compost under the soil for you. By merely spreading compost over existing garden beds and relaxing, you will allow the myriad colonies of earthworms in your yard to do their job. They are the foot soldiers of the garden. Within about six weeks they will have pulled the compost down into the subsoil and converted it into earthworm magic: castings.

3. **Add castings.** I mix one part worm castings with ten parts compost, and the results are undeniably much better than without the earthworm castings. This is garden magic: natural, organic, full of microbes, and good for everything that grows.

4. **Prepare the hole.** You will be digging holes for larger plants that also require soil preparation. Dig the hole wider than deep, as most roots spread horizontally. A hole that is three times as wide as the root mass of the plant and two times as deep is perfect. Backfill the hole with two-thirds soil and one-third compost and a scoop or two of worm castings, or purchase a quality premixed garden soil, and add one part worm castings to ten parts new soil. Do not backfill the hole using the existing soil if it is clay. If it is of reasonable quality to begin with, only add about one-third of it back into the hole by volume. Firm the soil mixture around the roots with your foot if it is a big plant or your hands if it is a small one.

5. **Plant high.** Trees and shrubs like to have water drain away from their roots, not down into them. Mound soil up to the root flare of the plant about thirty centimetres, using a combination of compost/soil.

And finally, think of building a house: would you do it without a foundation? Not here in Canada you wouldn't. You should not build a garden without proper—generous!—soil preparation, either. Simple as that.

Chapter 2

Unsung Garden Heroes

Man is rated the highest animal, at least among all animals who returned the questionnaire.

—Robert Brault

The road to prosperity in Canadian gardens is paved with new ideas and the elimination of some old ideas. The notion that we need to sanitize our gardens each autumn is now met with derision by the new Canadian gardener. Fact is, your garden needs all that duff material that we so often take to the curb.

Happily, we are changing, however slowly.

I was brushing up on my War of 1812 history the other day and was impressed to read that several hundred British and Canadian sailors marched from Halifax to Kingston during the first winter of the war. They were needed to support the new boats being built to fight the good fight on the Great Lakes. Imagine that: no decent roads, sleeping under the stars most nights, trudging through the snow most days by foot. They would have had the benefit of neither motorized transportation nor modern, waterproof footwear.

This story calls to mind the many people who do yeoman's service but seldom get thanks. Like the earthworms in your garden (who, for the purposes of this essay, are loosely categorized as "people," too).

I have stated before that it is a very good idea to rake the leaves off your lawn and onto your garden. The leaves will mat down with rain and the weight of snow and begin to break down into a quality layer of organic matter. Come spring, when temperatures reach ten degrees Celsius, the earthworms move up to the surface of the soil and, upon discovering a fine harvest of leaves, munch on them until they disappear.

Take a trip out to your garden on Canada Day, July 1 (in case you forgot), and I guarantee that evidence of your leaves will be gone.

So, what happens to them? Glad you asked.

A GIFT TO GARDENERS

Earthworms are part of a biotic community. They, along with centipedes, sowbugs, and a variety of other useful earthbound critters, provide an invaluable service. When earthworms arrive at the surface of the soil they consume the carbon- and nitrogen-rich fallen leaves (and leaf mould). These are mineralized by micro-organisms inside the earthworm's gut. As the leaves pass through the sophisticated digestive system of the worm they are converted into nitrogen-rich earthworm castings. As the worms move through the soil, sometimes as deep as a metre, they constantly leave these castings behind. They are a gift to the gardener and her plants.

THE MAGIC OF CASTINGS

The castings quickly stabilize and become resistant to chemical and physical degradation. They enhance the quality of your soil by stabilizing and storing nitrogen and carbon, until the microbes in the soil break them down.

As the worms move through your soil they open it up, essentially aerating it, making oxygen available to the roots of your plants. Every plant on Earth benefits from oxygen at its root zone.

With healthier roots, your plants will perform better, the need to fertilize is minimized (or it disappears), and water moves through the soil more efficiently. Plants more easily channel their roots through the tunnels created by the earthworms.

While we could assume that earthworms do their work as part of some big master plan on the part of Mother Nature, it is worthwhile noting that there are no native earthworms in Canada. If they existed at one time, as fossils suggest they did, they were wiped out by the last ice age. Your friendly neighbourhood earthworms are immigrants. Either they moved up here from the Deep South, where the glaciers never existed, or people brought them over here from Europe during the great plant-importing schemes of the 1700s through to 1940.

There are over one hundred types of earthworms in North America. Some are a nuisance, as prairie gardeners can tell you. There, they leave enormous mounds of castings on the surface of the soil. Growing a relatively flat lawn is all but impossible in Southern Alberta, for instance. But many other worm species do a lot of good.

To be practical about the matter, here is some information about how to nurture the worm population in your yard.

- They are moisture sensitive. During drought they move deep into the soil and enter a resting phase. In heavy rain they move to the surface of the soil to escape the lack of air in their tunnels.

- Avoid chemicals at all costs. Many chemicals are known to do permanent damage to earthworm populations (for example, carbaryl, malathion, diazinon).

- One active worm will process up to one-fifth of a kilogram of organic matter per year.

- Earthworms are hermaphrodites: they can self-propagate. The details of this activity could be raw material for a steamy novel that I would not want my name associated with. Google it.

- An earthworm can live between three and ten years, depending on species and soil conditions.

ANOTHER HERO OF THE GARDEN: THE COMMON TOAD

They feed on a wide variety of insects and have quite an appetite. You want to encourage toads as much as possible. The insects toads eat are often a nuisance in the garden. Slugs and mosquitoes are just two of their preferred prey.

They overwinter deep in the soil and will travel up to half a kilometre to reach a breeding ground come spring. Males often get a free ride on the back of a female. Perhaps we should make up a new expression, "couch toad," to describe certain males of the human species.

It takes about two years for a toad to mature to full size, but they live for up to ten years. To encourage a population of toads in your yard, I recommend that you leave some leaves on the soil (another reason to do this), do not sanitize your garden by removing all the perennials and mulch that is there in the autumn. Give them shelter and they will reward you next season.

Earthworms and toads are just two of the unsung heroes of the garden. Together they are essential weapons in our war against inferior-quality soil. They represent a natural element of the garden of the future. Nurture earthworms and toads, and you will belong to the select group of people that I call the new Canadian gardener.

Chapter 3
a Cure *for*
Plant Blindness

Man's heart away from nature becomes hard.

—Standing Bear (c. 1829–1908)

I live in the world of plants. I make my living here. And yet, there are times when even seasoned professionals don't see the plants for the sea of green that surrounds us. This story illustrates the challenge that we have, in the world of horticulture, to open the eyes of everyone to the wonders of plants and all that they represent.

Plant blindness is real. But a cure for it may be a sign of these times.

The notion that humans can be blind to the world of plants just never occurred to me, and then I had lunch with friends Allen Dennis and Denis Flanagan. As I think about this now, I am blown away. It started out innocently enough, with Allen explaining he had taken his grandchildren to a new aquarium over the weekend.

"It was amazing, and I would really recommend it," he gushed. "There are real sharks and a moving sidewalk that takes you on a tour under a glass aquarium full of fascinating fish." The kids evidently loved the place. Allen did too: "But you know, an hour and a half and I was done. Time to go home."

Denis, keen listener that he is, picked up on a brilliant idea. "Next time, why don't you take them to the Royal Botanical Gardens in Burlington? It is not just a flower garden. It is over two thousand acres, full of trails and wildlife and they have a lot of things for kids going on there every day."

Allen responded that he had never been to the "RBG," even though he lives in Burlington, its home town. "It just never occurred to me," he replied.

A light came on inside of my head, and I realized that the rumours are true: there is such a thing as "plant blindness," and it was in the room at that very moment, dwelling in the midst of three horticulturalists.

WHAT IS PLANT BLINDNESS?

In 1999, botanist-educators Elisabeth Schussler of the Ruth Patrick Science Education Center in Aiken, South Carolina, and James Wandersee of Louisiana State University coined the phrase "Plant Blindness" after observing that people prefer to view objects that are between one and fifteen degrees below eye level.

Digging deeper, they discovered that humans are predisposed to seeing many objects, but not plants. Other researchers had discovered that the eye generates over 10 million bits of data per second for visual processing, but the brain extracts only about forty bits and fully processes only the sixteen bits that reach our conscious attention.

The question that Wandersee and Schussler asked was, "How does the brain decide which 16 bits of visual information to focus on?" The results, simply put, pointed to objects that move, are of conspicuous colour or pattern, objects that are known, and objects that are potential threats. Since plants don't move (except on a windy day), they don't eat us, and they blend into the background, we just don't give them a lot of attention.

These findings bring to mind the many errant golf balls that I have searched for since taking up golf a few years ago. The more golf balls I lose, the more I find. Every time I venture out onto the golf course and take my usual (bad) swing, I train my eyes by the smallest of degrees to see the white, dimply ball. How I wish the rest of my game had improved as much as my ball-finding abilities.

Researchers generally define plant blindness as "the inability to see or notice the plants in one's own environment, leading to the inability to recognize the importance of plants in the biosphere and in human affairs." Plant blindness also comprises an "inability to appreciate the unique biological and aesthetic features of plants."

Our inability to appreciate plants leads to the prevalent opinion that plants are not relevant to us or the world around us. Do you see how this could be a problem? Consider, for just a moment, that all of the oxygen that we breathe is manufactured by the green, living world around us and suddenly a light might come on in your head, too. Like it did for my friend Allen who drove his grandchildren for forty minutes, from the "home of the Royal Botanical Gardens" in Burlington to downtown Toronto, through traffic delays, to pay an admission price that is more than twice that of the RBG. This picture does not make sense, until we view it through the prism of plant blindness.

Don't get me wrong, Toronto has long needed a first-class attraction that reflects the wonders of the aquatic world. I am not dishing on Ripley's. Rather, I would like to thank them for drawing to my attention the mountain of work that needs to be done to close the attention deficit gap where plants are concerned. The fact is, we humans are more attracted to animals than we are plants. The research does not say this, exactly, but anecdotally I conclude that we like animals more because we are members of their family (granted, it's a large family). We are not, however, plants. Nor do we want to be.

EDEN PROJECT

In 1999, when the calendar moved us from the last millennium into the new one, and we were preoccupied with whether our computers would work in the morning and if the world might, by some miscalculation, suddenly blow up, we woke to a bright, cold mid-winter morning, much like the one before it. The Britons, however, were busy filling in a hole that had taken them over 150 years to dig, with the world's largest greenhouse complex. Royal Doulton had been mining clay from the ground of Devon and no longer had a use for the resulting pit. Seeing an opportunity, a man named Tim Smit recruited the help of several expert horticulturalists and decided to create the Eden Project, sinking about $500 million into an attraction that celebrates the role of plants in our world and provides education to people of all ages.

I have visited the Eden Project on three occasions, in the company of three different people. Each one of my guests was equally impressed. "Who would think to invest *this* much in a public attraction that celebrates plants?" one of them exclaimed. I don't know, but I can report that the place was packed with tourists from near and far each time I attended. The Eden Project is a world-class zoo for plants.

I would recommend that you visit the Eden Project the next time you find yourself on the other side of the Atlantic. I also recommend that you visit the Royal Botanical Gardens: one of the great, underrated public hot spots in Canada. For that matter, I recommend *all* botanical gardens to you as logical places to start your journey in exploring the wonderful world of plants. Perhaps we can reduce the prevalence of plant blindness one attraction at a time.

Chapter 4

What We Can Learn
from the British

If you have a library and a garden,
you want for nothing else.

—British saying

The future of Canadian gardening is mirrored, to some extent, by what we see in Britain. In my experience, the evolution of gardening in the UK provides a crystal ball for the garden we will experience here in the future.

Here are some observations from the world's most famous garden that inform us about the meaning of gardening tomorrow.

There is a 250-year-old maple tree on the original four-hectare grounds of Kew Gardens in London, England, that attracts a lot of attention. It is the only maple tree I have ever seen that is fenced in, held up with supports made of iron, bricks, and mortar. Shortly after marrying King George III, Queen Charlotte had this maple planted. It is less beautiful than it is symbolic.

Walking through the 121 hectares that constitute Kew Gardens today, it is hard to believe that this horticultural treasure was ever anything other than spectacular. Indeed, Kew has been designated a World Heritage Site by UNESCO. Truth is, of course, that it has evolved just as all living things evolve. Kew Gardens is not anything like the Kew of old. Gardening is, I am reminded, an art form that is in a constant state of change. The art of creating botanical gardens is like private gardens in this regard.

I have yet to meet a gardener, Canadian or otherwise, who has determined that their work is done. Unlike a painting or sculpture, you do not just walk away from your work when you garden; you nurture it and work with the tools at hand—including the limitations imposed by Mother Nature—to create something beautiful.

TODAY'S BEAUTY IS TOMORROW'S HISTORY

It is the changes in the British habits of gardening that intrigue me. I do not need to argue in favour of their gardening pedigree. No nation on Earth has invested in the discipline of gardening to the extent and with the enthusiasm of the Brits. It is their five hundred–year history of complete devotion to gardening—bordering at times on mania—which speaks for itself.

I first toured British gardens some forty years ago. Since then, I have witnessed dramatic changes in their approach to gardening, and I believe that we can learn from them.

NATURE, NOT NURTURE

Years ago, a British gardener may have suggested that no garden is worth having without the proper care and maintenance. Today the same thing holds true, but the standards have changed.

Take "naturalizing,"' for example. During my recent tour of British gardens, I could not help but notice that the clipped and manicured lawn has been replaced in many corners of the public show garden with areas where a mixture of grass and perennial flowering plants have been allowed to grow up and go to seed. Many of the new meadows provide nectar and pollen for bees, butterflies, and other pollinators. Carefully planned perhaps, but not manicured as British gardens of the past. The sound of a lawn mower is conspicuously absent.

In recent years an all but ignored corner of Kew Gardens has become a big attraction: the Woodland Walk is carved from a naturalized portion of a long-established hardwood bush. Many of the trees that once lived there and have fallen simply rot. Signs are used to educate visitors about the benefits of rot and decay. One sign posts an explanation:

> *Why don't we remove our dead trees?*
> *Because dead wood is vitally important in keeping a woodland healthy.*
> *Because dead wood is recycled back into the soil.*
> *Because as wood rots, it provides homes and food for thousands of species.*
> *The movement to "natural" is powerful and it is felt worldwide.*

Even on Canadian golf courses. Audubon provides certification to golf courses across North America. This certificate comes with stringent conditions that include the creation of naturalized areas to attract songbirds and other wildlife. If you are a golfer, you will no doubt have seen signs in the rough, stating that the area is "out of bounds" as ball retrieval disturbs the wildlife nurtured there. Just a few years ago, such an idea would have seemed absurd.

CIVIC PRIDE

Britain in Bloom is a countrywide competition that encourages the planting of flowers, permanent landscaping, and services that enhance life in the community. The program has been in existence for about forty-eight years and was the inspiration behind our own Communities in Bloom program, which has run successfully for over twenty years. Both programs are designed to encourage the demonstration of civic pride and celebrate it wherever possible.

WILDLIFE

The British love of animals is well known. Is it any wonder that Doctor Dolittle, the vet who could talk to the animals, had an English accent in film adaptations of Hugh Lofting's literary works? More recently, we have seen protection for such creatures as toads and turtles by building tunnels and causeways specifically for them under roadways.

A recent issue of *Kew* magazine, the garden's official publication, dedicated 30 per cent of its space to news about wildlife. The *London Times* provides a daily "Nature News" report in the main section of the paper. In one recent summer edition there were four paragraphs devoted to the arrival of the tortoiseshell butterfly. Perhaps someday we will see Canadian wildlife featured prominently and regularly in the pages of a daily newspaper. Lord knows that we have enough of it—wildlife, that is.

ALLOTMENTS

Anyone who has spent any time in Britain knows of the love of allotment gardens. Much more than a place to grow food, the allotment craze provides entire weekends of entertainment for whole families. Rather than driving up north to the trailer or cottage as many of us do, Britons see fit to scoot over to the allotment to set up camp. Entertainment is found in the activity of staking tomatoes, pulling weeds, and enjoying some Pimm's in the shade while bragging about the size of one's courgette. Or whatever.

Here in Canada, the interest in public garden plots is also growing substantially. Not only are we claiming a few square metres of otherwise wasted space for our own, but many are teaming up with whole communities to plant and maintain food gardens where the harvest is shared equally among the participants.

CHANGING FOCUS

Gardeners are no longer interested in plants for plants' sake, but rather the new passion for them springs from a desire to create habitat for wildlife, to put quality food on the table, to bring communities together through shared gardens, and it provides a convenient reason to be social. Yes, gardening can cure shyness. And these gardens are flourishing coast to coast, from the Sooke Community Garden in British Columbia to the Hope Blooms Community Garden in North End Halifax, Nova Scotia.

A tree that was planted around 1760 is worth preserving if for no other reason than to remind us that a mere four-hectare plant collection has morphed into the greatest botanical garden in the world, where three hundred people are employed in medical research. From this point of view, the future looks exciting, indeed.

a Wealth of Bees

*Look deep into nature, and then
you will understand everything better.*

—Albert Einstein (1879–1955)

This story took a long time to write. About forty years.

The image in my mind of a "perfect garden" is a thing of beauty for all its imperfection. Not only do I realize that rot and decay are my friends, as they support the beneficial wildlife activity that I dream about, but also the garden is suddenly alive with activity that I never could dream about.

Canadians are being forced by the twenty- and thirtysomethings to think of the garden differently. And to a large degree, we can thank the decline of the honeybee for the information that has saturated news channels in recent years. Without their decline we would not likely have started in this new direction.

✿

Curious thing, this gardening business. It is always changing. My career has been steeped in gardening for as long as I can remember. When I was a kid, my dad quizzed my four siblings and me on Sunday afternoons by asking us to identify plants in our garden. A nickel for every correct answer. A dime for the correct botanical name. I was lousy at this game, as I always seemed to have something else on my mind, like street hockey or bike riding.

Quizzing my own children about plant names was one of those things that I vowed I would never do. Which is why I received a text message from my eldest last week, asking me what to do with the dogwood she had just purchased, which turned out to be a boxwood. While she got half of the name right and they both produce wood if you let them grow for long enough, I was tempted to shed a tear for her late grandpa. No doubt he would be proud of her, for reasons other than her plant knowledge. No nickel or dime for her.

THANKS TO NEW GARDENERS

This incoming generation of gardeners is fascinating. They know what they want, and a rose garden is not on the list. Instead they are interested in gardening as it relates to the environment and food. They get their knees dirty all right, in efforts to grow healthy food and make a positive contribution to the green, living world around us.

The many questions that people ask about the decline in the native bee population spring from the concerns that we hear expressed by the twenty- and thirtysomethings who are venturing out into their own gardens, many for the first time.

Suffice it to say that there are many misconceptions about native Canadian bees, and their role in the plant world and our own. Here are some key facts that might help clear things up for you, whatever age you may bee (sorry, the pun is irresistible):

I am reminded of a neighbour of ours who stopped me on Main Street in our nearby town early this spring and asked where he could buy milkweed seeds (the answer is Home Hardware). What is interesting is that my buddy Doug would not have planted milkweed a few years ago. He has learned recently that the native monarch butterfly population is in decline due to the overly effective control of milkweed by humans. Proof that it pays to be beautiful, as the monarch surely is, if you need a helping hand from people. This works for pandas and whales too. If you're not ready to plant common milkweed, try the less pervasive butterfly weed or red milkweed or any of the other milkweed species (just make sure you do some research into their spreading behaviour and necessary growing conditions).

HOW YOU CAN HELP

Attracting more native bees to your yard is not all that hard, when you turn your mind to it. Here are some tips:

❧ **Grow more native plants.** There is a lot of enthusiasm for planting natives in the home landscape, and as a result, many garden retailers are doing an excellent job of making them available. Look for native flowering shrubs like serviceberry and sumac; native woodland plants, like trilliums and mayflower, are now nursery grown. There are many native perennials as well that perform well in our gardens, including Echinacea (purple cone flower) and yarrow.

❧ **Install mason bee houses.** There are several native mason bees that are already living in your neighbourhood. Why not provide habitat to attract more? All you need are some pre-drilled mason nesting boxes, mounted no more than 140 cm off the ground, facing east or south (out of the wind and afternoon sun).

❧ **Build an insect hotel.** It is easy to build an insect hotel, mostly from the stuff you have in the yard and garage that is otherwise useless. Remember that bees and other beneficial insects enjoy a garden that is in a state of "managed disrepair" (I made this expression up). This is another way of saying that a sanitized garden—where the fallen leaves, debris, and other stuff that detracts from our image of the perfect garden have been blown away by a leaf blower— is just not acceptable for them. You want beneficial insects in your yard? You must create habitat that works for them, not you. A five-star hotel experience for a bumblebee looks like the gardener went on a long vacation.

I predict that Canadians will have as many insect hotels and mason bee houses in their yards in twenty years as we have bird feeders now. Watch!

And how do I know this? I have seen the other side. With a daughter living in London, England, I have the perfect excuse to travel to the UK a few times a year and while there I visit public gardens and retail garden centres. There, I see almost as many insect habitat devices as bird feeders. And the Britons love their birds! In this case, I believe that we will learn from Britons and we will learn from our own experience that creating wildlife habitat in our yards is fun, productive, and entertaining.

🌱 **Let your perennials stand.** This autumn allow your ornamental grasses, rudbeckia and Joe Pye weed, etc., to stand over the winter. The hollow stems and 'debris' that accumulate at their base provide needed habitat and protection for many bees.

Alas, we are changing, but ever so slowly. Our urban sensibilities and ideas about what make a yard and garden beautiful is a work in progress. Thank goodness for the youngsters.

Chapter 6

Think *like a* Hummingbird

The moon quotes the sun, the rivers quote the trees,
and trees quote the breeze.

—Terri Guillemets

As you read this story, you may wonder what its practical advice has to do with the changing nature of the Canadian garden experience. While I offer some useful advice for the gardener who wants to attract beneficial wildlife, I want to push the boundaries of your thinking. When is a hedge much more than a living fence? When is a vine more than a grape plant that provides fruit? If we take the time to think like a hummingbird, we begin to see the garden as a very different place.

Take a moment to think of your property, even your condo balcony, as something much greater than the boundaries indicated on a survey. Think of the piece of real estate that you live on as a pearl in a necklace that extends down your street, around the corner, and beyond. This necklace is a circle or oval that has no end. Round and round it goes. Now you are beginning to think like a bee or a hummingbird. A visit to the flowering plants in your yard leads to more on the other side of your fence, which leads to permanent tree cover where birds and insects build nests (habitat), which leads to a nearby source of water.

There is much that you can do in your yard and garden that impacts the beneficial wildlife in your entire community. Here are a few ideas that might spark your interest and your desire to play a bigger role in the world of pollinators that exists right outside of your back door.

🌱 **Plant a hedge.** The fence is a fine thing for creating privacy in your yard. A fence provides privacy while sunbathing or reading quietly. However, a permanent hedge can provide so much more, while offering privacy and quiet (*more* quiet, as it absorbs noise more effectively than a fence). A living wall—or hedge—is often home to nesting birds and shelter for insects and small creatures that are part of the natural web. I prefer native white cedar as a hedge in a sunny position for fast growth and a permanent vertical delineator between neighbours. Other great hedging plants include the classic deciduous privet (up to two metres high), boxwood to zone 5 (up to a metre high), alpine currant (two metres high, great for the shade), and for an informal approach to the project, plant any flowering shrub that you like. For instance, a few lilacs lined up in a row make an effective barrier that will come alive with wildlife as it grows.

🌱 **Lift a slab.** Do you have a flagstone, interlocking, or patio-slab walkway or patio? Consider lifting some random pieces out of the puzzle and fill them in with low-growing "stepables." These are ground-hugging plants that attract pollinators while in bloom and provide safety for small, ground-dwelling insects. Look for creeping thyme (*Thymus serpyllum*) for a great show of colour early in summer, Irish or Scotch moss or any number of low-growing sedums and sempervivums. All bloom at one point in the season and tolerate a moderate amount of foot traffic. They cool down an otherwise hot area in the yard too.

"**Cut and come again.**" Near the end of July, I cut my veronica (about fifty of them) in half. They bloomed earlier in the month and now they are ready to bloom again, but only if I take the time to remove the first flush of flowers. The same is true for many early summer flowering perennials, including sweet william, Echinops (globe thistles), lavender, and delphiniums. While the second coming of bloom is generally not as dramatic as the first, it is worth the effort. Pollinators will thank you for it. Pinch the main flower out of butterfly bush after it has bloomed to encourage more lateral blossoms late in August and September.

❧ **Plant a wall.** The fences and walls around your property come alive when you plant a vine to grow up them. I can't imagine anything more beautiful than a clematis and climbing rose planted together against a fence or on a trellis, secured to the garage wall. Or a flowering hydrangea clinging to shaded support. Birds nest in vines and enjoy the fruits of many like pyracantha (firethorn); native Virginia creeper and even grapes cool an area down.

❧ **Leave it standing.** Ornamental grasses, rudbeckia, Echinacea (purple coneflower), monarda (bee balm), and Shasta daisy all produce a seed head, once they finish blooming, that attracts foraging songbirds: don't cut them down. The flocks of yellow finches that invade my garden from now through winter are testament to this. Come autumn, resist the temptation to sanitize your garden and let these perennials stand.

Speaking of autumn, one of the best choices you can make when considering beneficial wildlife in your yard is leaving the fallen leaves in it. (I can't emphasize this helpful measure enough!) Rake leaves off your lawn as they can do damage there. Moving them under hedges, onto perennial beds, and even onto the veggie garden where they will rot down before the next growing season, adds much-needed organic raw material to the soil and habitat for ground-dwelling insects.

Less work for you, more beneficial to the "beneficials."

Easy!

Chapter 7

Bring *on* *the* Critters

Life is really simple,
but we insist on making it complicated.

—Confucius (551 BC–479 BC)

The natural world surrounds us. We live near it but not in it, except when we are camping. And we develop attitudes toward the native habitants in our natural surroundings based on some not-so-scientific information. And sometimes we fuss ourselves into excess work based on our biases. Like getting rid of squirrels. Or worse, getting rid of squirrels while trying to feed the birds. Now that is a wonderful way to become a laughingstock in your natural environment!

I have a solution....

You may not like what I'm about to say, but, "Bring on the critters."

If you happen to be fortunate enough to find yourself in Invermere, British Columbia, any time soon, you will notice that every tree on the main street has a wire cage around it. These have been installed at great expense to taxpayers to prevent deer damage. It is difficult to have a garden in Invermere, as the deer there have developed a palate for just about every living thing with leaves. Even the list of "deer-resistant plants" that I offer on my website (markcullen.com/search-the-library) is pretty much useless in Invermere.

Squirrels have this in common with deer, I find. When they are finished eating everything in sight that comes naturally to them, they start chowing down and destroying many of the plants that are not normally on their menu. "Why is a red squirrel ripping the bark off my mature sugar maple?" one reader asked. My answer: "I have no idea." To get the answer, you would have to get inside the brain of a squirrel, and I am just not interested enough in the subject to become a full-time neuro-student of squirrels.

I say, "Garden calm and carry on." With apologies to my British friends.

I do not have deer and only the occasional rabbit in my garden. I hear the horror stories about them when I travel, mostly outside of the densely populated urban centres of the country and into the small towns and rural areas. While on a speaking engagement in Muskoka, Ontario, recently, I took questions from the audience. The enquiries about deer damage quickly became a theme of the evening. "Everyone with a deer problem, there is a special meeting afterwards. We will sit in a circle and have a deer therapy session," I suggested. It got a laugh, but we did not meet afterwards, and there were no definitive answers to this dilemma.

This story is not for deer victims. It is for the more urban set that wake up to raccoon scat on the patio or skunk smells where they were grubbing for grubs in the lawn. I know your frustration with rodents, as many of them are dumped at the end of our driveway at our country property north of the city. You want racoons, skunks, and squirrels? We have them in spades. Many are "city rodents." We can tell because they act confused: raccoons wander around in the daytime looking for shelter, and squirrels are chased around by their more local, native cousins. They look lost because they are, but they do precious little damage. They seem to be a nuisance when we pay too much attention to them.

There are many critters that we tend to demonize. For instance, bats do not advertise well. We have many notions about them that are not grounded in fact. While they can carry rabies, that is less likely than with ground-dwelling rodents and coyotes. They may bite if you corner one, but I cannot find reports of them biting people in Canada. Ever. Bats voraciously consume flying insects. They can consume enough mosquitoes to equal their body weight in one evening. Bat populations are generally in decline and that is too bad: we need more native bats.

Snakes get a bad rap, too. I have no idea why. I think that the story about the Garden of Eden did them a poor service and set them up to fail in the public relations department. Perhaps the fact that they are cold-blooded and crawl on their belly is a turnoff for some people. The truth is they control mice and large insects like slugs, earwigs, grubs, and the like quite effectively. What is not to like, except they aren't cute.

Chipmunks are cute. And we are overrun with them. This summer, they have burrowed with abandon under the locust tree in my backyard. They run and jump and skip and play, chasing each other like identical twins with way too much energy. Sometimes they make us laugh out loud. Any damage that occurs in our yard due to excess chipmunk activity is forgiven because they are cute.

You know what aren't cute? Coyotes. They come over to our place most evenings and howl at the moon and each other between midnight and four in the morning, often right under our bedroom window. Coyotes are like the screaming baby that is not satisfied by a bottle of warm milk: they just seem to enjoy howling. Coyotes are the reason why I yawn a lot midafternoon this time of year. They may also be the reason why I don't have deer or rabbit problems in my garden. Perhaps I should send a few of them to Invermere.

Part II

FOOD PROSPERITY and BUILDING COMMUNITY

Am I the only one who looks at a vegetable garden as a thing of beauty? After the frost leaves the cold Canadian ground, and gardeners finally get out to "work the soil," I really like the musky smell that permeates the air. In my nearly half hectare of vegetables, the tree swallows arrive in the first week of April to bed down among my forty nesting boxes. It is a thrill to see them, to hear their songs, and to watch them pair off as if attending a high school dance.

The odours, sights, and sounds add a dimension to my gardening experience that is not unique to the edibles. My pollinator gardens and meadows are similar. What the food garden adds to my gardening experience is something extraordinary. It is the only place where plants are arranged in straight lines: raspberries supported by horizontal wires set a metre high, asparagus in its ferny patch, and virtually everything else in the garden lined up like soldiers.

My vegetable garden is a place of order, where I know each plant like I know my children. I tend it with doting precision, weeding in rhythm to the swing of my arms and the bend in my back. It is the place that I go most summer evenings after dinner. I can think there. And dream.

It is the place that produces a bounty that I can share. I grow over two hundred tomato plants and fifty pepper plants. Last year I grew several hundred leeks, and no, I didn't name them all. They are not *that* much like my children!

You might ask why. With only two people living in our house, and even with an extended family of kids, in-laws, and grandbabies, there is a limit to how much produce they want, even when it is free.

I take the excess to the local food bank. They seem grateful for the donation, and I get a warm, fuzzy feeling every time I visit to deliver fresh, free produce for people who generally don't get much free food that is truly good for them. And sharing this bounty of edibles goes a long way toward building community.

I am an organic gardener. When we brought our first baby home over thirty years ago, I looked at her, considered my responsibilities as a new parent, and gave the chemicals that were hiding in my tool shed to my grateful father, who raised a family of five kids with many chemicals around the house and garage. Different generation, different standards.

And now, a new generation enters the stage once again. My son, Ben, and my three daughters enjoy planting veggies and herbs, but they use containers more than I ever did. And they like heritage veggies, ones that have been around for over a hundred years or more. They would never even think of using garden chemicals, and they talk about their most recent veggie garden experiences more than I ever did. My two daughters with kids of their own feed their children food from their garden whenever they can: it is their food of first choice.

My food garden is a place of joy. Giving produce away and sequestering some time out of my day to go there and think, these are fringe benefits. The real value to the food gardening experience, in my opinion, is the miracle that occurs every time a seed germinates and grows into a plant that serves my human purpose, of fuel from food.

Food from the soil? A bizarre concept for anyone who knows only the sterile environment of a grocery store: Styrofoam plates wrapped in cellophane. And now, portion cut so that all you have to do is rinse the produce under a tap and put it on a plate. I prefer my own reality, thank you very much. And I consider it a thing of beauty.

As you read part two, I hope you will agree that food from the garden is a new measure of prosperity—with both tangible and intangible benefits.

Chapter 8

Stop, *in the* Name *of* Food

Never underestimate the power of a good meal.

—Nick Saul and Andrea Curtis, *The STOP: How the Fight for Good Food Transformed a Community and Inspired a Movement*

Gardeners are "social engagers." This means that the activity of gardening brings people together. Not just on planting day, but every day that a community garden needs tending.

One of the fascinating aspects of gardening today is the integration of generations and cultures in a food garden. This story illustrates the power of public community gardens where a collaborative approach is taken.

This is not easy, as you are about to learn. But it is enormously effective.

As my late father used to say, "Anything worth doing is worth doing well." And doing this well takes a lot of effort and planning.

In an editorial for Toronto's the *Star* on February 22, 2014, Debbie Field, executive director of FoodShare Toronto, wrote in with her "big idea": "What if Toronto agreed to put first in planning, urban design and social policy…fresh fruits and vegetables within a 15 minute walk of everyone's home?"

Ms. Field imagines an urban environment where people are knit together through a common interest in food. Not just an interest in filling our tummies, but locally grown, homegrown, always fresh, accessible food that would be used to prepare meals that reflect the rich, deep, and complex cultural mosaic that makes up Toronto.

The truth? The raw material already exists for just such an endeavour.

FRESH, ACCESSIBLE FOOD

Recently, I acquired a copy of a powerful book titled *The STOP: How the Fight for Good Food Transformed a Community and Inspired a Movement.* It is a fascinating read. The authors, Nick Saul and Andrea Curtis, dramatically changed my view of food as it relates to the economically disadvantaged in the city.

The story begins with personal reflections on Nick's responsibilities as the manager of a large food bank in the west end of Toronto. As food was meted out to recipients in need each day, he experienced an unsettling feeling in his stomach. How was this changing the lives of The Stop clients? Was this food bank just dumping food into a bottomless pit of demand? Was it any different than other food banks in the country? Where was the progress? Where was the dignity in reaching out each week for free food?

While being careful to defend and support the idea of food banks, Mr. Saul takes us on a journey that he and his team have been on for twenty years. He exposes the frustrations of handing out food for free and discovering how clients didn't want to be poor and were never even remotely ambivalent about their circumstances. He learned that "they cared deeply about their homes, their lives and a better future for themselves and their kids."

Mr. Saul explains, "The food bank experience is so often a slow, painful death of the spirit—forcing yourself to visit a crowded, ill-equipped, makeshift place, answer personal questions, swallow your pride as you wait in a lineup. Reaching the front of the line only to be offered bizarre processed food products or slimy, wilted lettuce that couldn't be revived with electric shock treatment is the final nail in the coffin." All of this suggested to Mr. Saul that there was a better way to meet the needs of the many hungry people in our urban setting.

When the Metcalf Foundation supported the "Income Security Council," a program to explore the possibilities of increasing assistance to the underprivileged in the city, one woman attending a public meeting stood up and said, "'My name is Jane, and I'm a drain on the system.'" These words focused attention on one of the biggest problems with food banks: people who are forced to use them do not feel dignified by the experience of putting out their hand for free food.

The STOP book provides a very practical example of one person's journey of discovery as Nick Saul seeks answers to the burning questions that relate to providing access to healthy food for all. This journey did not take place in a straight line. Perhaps, if someone had been able to show Mr. Saul the way, someone who had asked the same questions years before and discovered the answers, then the road would have been less bumpy.

Alas, whenever we blaze new ground there are surprises. The book is full of them, including some struggles that illuminate the complexities of the process. Bringing people together to collaborate on such a critical question as *How do we make healthy food accessible to everyone?* will stir up a mixture of responses. And, as the book relates, it most certainly does.

ARTSCAPE WYCHWOOD BARNS

One of the answers to the question evolved as The Stop sought a new home. The idea was to provide a place where people would not just receive a food handout but would also learn how to prepare it for the table, preserve it for off-season consumption, and have access to ground on which to grow their own.

Located in a century-old bus and street car–repair building, and in more affluent part of Toronto than they had been previously, the Green Barn at Wychwood Barns, a public space dedicated to honouring the local artists' community, provided the perfect site for illustrating the connection between all the players in the food system. Today it features a large teaching garden and greenhouse for locals. Saul reflects, "I often field phone calls and emails from exasperated friends and educators who want their adolescent children to volunteer in The Stop programs. They say their middle-class kids have no idea about their own privilege. Because they never see anyone living any other way. Their kids are isolated in a bubble of entitlement. These well-meaning people want their children to see how others live so that they will appreciate all that they have." He explains that The Stop does not have a rehab program for privileged kids. They have a stringent application process in place for volunteers, through which the whole experience of sharing food is honoured and clients are treated with respect.

There are barriers between the have and have-nots where food is concerned. Within these barriers all kinds of misunderstandings can fester. The shared experience of growing food, sharing it, and advocating for access to it for all is "a great equalizer" according to Saul.

In her editorial, Debbie Field asks us to imagine community gardens, composting, bake ovens, beekeeping, fruit trees, and urban farms added to schools, parks, roofs, and balconies of buildings.

Imagine, indeed. Truth is, we need not imagine any longer. Such a system exists in microcosm: The Stop, Artscape Wychwood Barns, and hundreds of community and allotment gardens that already operate across the country and beyond are testament to the fact that there is life and dignity beyond food banks.

Chapter 9

Local Food *for* Everyone

Food cannot be disentangled from social relationships.

—Nick Saul, Community Food Centres Canada

My friend and colleague Lorraine Johnson once said, "If we took all of the space in the city of Toronto where food could be grown and grew food on it, we could feed ourselves."

What you should know about Lorraine is that she does not speak off the top of her head. Especially when she writes. (And I love her writing!) She made this statement after much research into the subject, which formed the foundation of her book *The Gardener's Manifesto* (it is not nearly as ponderous as the title suggests).

Yes. A city can feed itself with a plan and the collective will to do it. This story suggests how.

How can a city feed itself? Can local food be made available to every citizen regardless of their income and access to transportation? Is it possible to eliminate the need for food banks in our cities? Can we grow our own food in the urban environment? These questions are contemplated every day by people who are active in organizations that are working toward answers.

Truth is, we have options. As I researched the background for this story, I became excited by the enormous number of resources that are at our doorstep and the future prospects for more intensive efforts to feed ourselves with healthy, locally grown food. It seems that the issues connected to locally produced food are all over the media. *Municipal World* magazine caters to municipal councillors, mayors, and staff. Recently they featured a cover story and in-depth article about the "local food economy." In this article they recount these numerous encouraging stories:

- Thousands of raised vegetable boxes built on unused parking spaces in downtown Vancouver produced over 45,000 kilograms of fresh vegetables and supported 150 youth last year.

- Retired basketball star Will Allen turned a derelict plant nursery into a food production super-centre that produces over $500,000 worth of produce, meat, and fish, and employs sixty-five staff in Milwaukee, Wisconsin.

- The *Garden* magazine in the UK reports that a grant of more than $1.5 million is helping every London school grow their own food. It is intended that the project will become the model for a national food-growing scheme.

- In Toronto, non-profit Food Share serves 150,000 customers and generates over $2 million in revenue annually from its fresh produce delivery service, school programs, community kitchen, catering activities, and café. Debbie Field, the former executive director of FoodShare, kicked off this discussion in the *Toronto Star* when she made a submission to our "Big Ideas" for the city contest.

HOW ARE WE FEEDING OURSELVES LOCALLY?

Many people are caught up in the question, *How can we provide access to locally produced food for all?* I think the more pressing question is, *How can we use the systems already in place to roll out a greater quantity of food to people who need it most?*

Evergreen Brick Works is located in the Don Valley ravine of Toronto, only a short bike ride from the high-end shopping district at Bloor and Yonge Streets. During a stroll through the Brick Works, I was exposed to an inspirational bevy of brochures and discussion with many of the movers and shakers in the local food movement. Orlando Martin López Gómez, for instance, was manning the FoodShare booth during a recent visit. His job title is "compost facilitator" and he is passionate about his subject. According to Orlando Gómez, the road to a healthy diet is paved with rotten vegetables and yard waste (not his words exactly, but close). In other words, if we composted as much organic waste as we throw out, we could grow enough food in that compost to feed ourselves. Imagine!

YOUNG URBAN FARMERS

If you are interested in feeding yourself using locally produced food, I recommend that you check out Young Urban Farmers in your town or city. "Fresh food from your yard without the work!" is the slogan for the organization of the same name in Toronto.

If you are a residential landowner, all you have to do is provide access to your own backyard this summer by letting the "young farmers" convert your dirt into a "thriving garden with a variety of heirloom vegetables for your family and community." The two key points: unfettered access to your yard and a willingness to share the bounty with the community, including the young farmers themselves. What a great idea! See cultivatetoronto.com/landsharer for further details.

FOOD BASKETS TO YOUR DOOR

Let's say that you don't have a yard to donate or you just don't want to donate the one that you have. How would you like to receive a bag of eight to twelve diverse types of produce every week at your front door? The people at Fresh City Farms provide such a service. As much as 80 per cent of the produce they sell is produced locally, year round, and it is never flown in. They also provide clinics to educate you on subjects that include organic urban gardening, balcony gardening, and garden planning and design. And, one of my personal favourites, "Mastering the Art of Composting and Soil Nutrition." (Details atfreshcityfarms.com.)

Speaking of food baskets, FoodShare produces food boxes that they make accessible to "Toronto communities and particularly prioritizing low-income people." This is part of a major, complex system of food growth, acquisition from local sources, and distribution at FoodShare. Fifteen volunteers come to their warehouse every week to pack up to 1,500 boxes for this purpose. While the cost per box is $18, the "supermarket" value is between $25 and $27, depending on the store and time of year. FoodShare is a United Way–supported organization. (Details at foodshare.net.)

COMMUNITY FOOD CENTRES

Nick Saul, co-author of *The STOP*, has graduated from the daily bump and grind of the food bank business to create a new organization called Community Food Centres Canada. He is using his extensive lessons learned at The Stop to fulfill the primary goal of this new organization: to drive the development of fifteen food centres across Canada in the next few years.

According to their brochure, "A community food centre is a welcoming space where people come together to grow, cook, share and advocate for good food. They provide emergency access to high-quality food in a dignified setting that doesn't compromise people's self-worth." Each centre features cooking, gardening, a common space where "community members find a common voice," and many opportunities to enhance their food skills from garden to fork. There are now eight Community Food Centres across the country, including Calgary, Alberta; Winnipeg, Manitoba; Perth, Stratford, and Hamilton, and two in Toronto, Ontario; and Dartmouth, Nova Scotia. (Details at cfccanada.ca.)

WEALTH IN KNOWLEDGE

Finding answers to the many prevalent questions associated with food access is not easy. But then, no one suggested that it would be.

Key words that keep cropping up in my research include:

- **Dignity.** As in, everyone is equally worthy of access to good food.
- **Shared experience.** Each of us has something useful to contribute to the effort for the benefit of all.
- **Better health.** Access to food is about access to nutritional food, especially fresh produce.
- **Empowerment.** Participants in the process feel better about themselves and their community.
- **Greater wealth.** We are a wealthier community when we make quality, fresh food more accessible to all.

Well, I added the part about the greater wealth. Much is lamented about the low-income parts of our cities. We have this habit of measuring wealth strictly in monetary terms. However, as anyone who has been hungry and learned to feed themselves can tell you, there can be wealth in abundance from the experience and knowledge of growing food, wealth that can be shared and multiplied without a nickel changing hands.

Chapter 10

Imagine Food Libraries

Someone has to stand up and say the answer isn't another pill. The answer is spinach.

—Bill Maher, 2007

I invite you to think for a moment about your local library. I trust that you have one accessible, if you live in a town or city in Canada. Libraries are, after all, an institution that we have come to expect in every corner of the country.

Now imagine that a library of food is located down the street from where you live. Well, not exactly a library, but a place where quality, locally grown food is available for all, like the books in your local library. And it is not a food bank, but a place where you can experience the growing and preparation of food. You can learn how to do these things at this place.

Nick Saul is one of my heroes, and I think of him whenever I dream about the future of the Canadian gardening experience. I study the words he uses as they help to inform me about where we are going with this gardening thing in terms of our overall health, and socially, as we become connected through the gardening experience. I reflect on words like *dignity*, *belonging*, and *equality*. These words help to sum up the modern image of my Canada. Does Nick's vision fit with the country that you want to be a part of in the future?

❧

During the winter and summer months, gardeners in Canada experience some hammock time. It is neither planting nor harvest time in the garden, so we enjoy the luxury of entering a special zone. A time when we can think more freely, a time to imagine.

I have been in touch with Nick Saul, the president and CEO of Community Food Centres (CFC) Canada. And no, this is not a new grocery store chain, but a national non-profit that's building vibrant, food-focused spaces in low-income communities. CFC is a relatively new organization that strives to make quality food accessible to all Canadians. It is an ambitious dream, but one that is coming true, one step at a time.

I had the pleasure of interviewing the visionary Nick Saul, and I'm happy to share our conversation here.

Nick, what are Community Food Centres and where are they?
Community Food Centres are dignified, welcoming spaces that bring people together to grow, cook, share, and advocate for good food for all. Each Community Food Centre offers a mix of programs that strive to increase access to healthy food, build food skills, and provide peer support and education and engagement opportunities. The exact program mix is determined by the needs of each community. Every Community Food Centre has the same goals: to build better health, skills, connection, and belonging in the low-income communities that need it most.

There are eight established or developing Community Food Centres in Canada: in Toronto, Hamilton, Stratford, Perth in Ontario; Dartmouth, Nova Scotia; Winnipeg Manitoba; Calgary Alberta.

Through our Good Food Organizations program, we're also supporting ninety organizations in fifty-six cities with grants and resources that help them offer healthy and dignity-focused programs in their communities.

What are the benefits of the Community Food Centre concept?

The idea of dignity through food is foremost in my mind these days. Dignity, belonging, and equality. We believe that people who have less shouldn't be made to feel the lesser for it. And that a good meal cooked with care and eaten with others can be the beginning of many amazing things.

We measure our impact in a number of areas: better access to healthy food, better food skills and physical health, better social connection and mental health, and better civic engagement. We want to work with our communities to push for public policies that support people to live safe, healthy, and hopeful lives.

Can you talk about the profound changes that can happen when people come together to grow their own food, learn how to prepare it, and to celebrate it together?

The power of food is something we see at our centres every day. Because food is this incredible thing. When you eat it together, you grow community and connection. Through it you can express your culture and your background. If you eat good food it energizes you and keeps you healthy. When you grow food sustainably, it nourishes the soil and increases the health of our planet. And when everyone has access to good food, you have inclusive, connected, and equitable communities. That's the vision we are igniting across Canada through our work.

What is the future of that work? Where is it leading?

Building welcoming places that meet people where they're at and that provide engaging ways to eat healthier, meet friends, and get involved in improving their neighbourhoods and circumstances is more important now than ever. We see a future where every community has a Community Food Centre, just like every community has a library. There will always be a role for places that bring people together and create ways for them to get engaged in their communities.

The future we see is a Canada where everyone eats well. We need a bold re-imagining of the role food plays in our lives. In low-income communities for certain, and for all Canadians.

(For details of their work go to cfccanada.ca.)

PLANT A ROW, GROW A ROW

It is worth reflecting on the value of sharing our resources with others who do not have access to fresh, healthy Canadian-grown (i.e. local) food. A volunteer-driven program started in Winnipeg in the 1980s, when Ron and Eunice O'Donovan had excess potatoes from their backyard garden and donated them to their local food bank. An idea was born, and the rest is history.

I urge you to consider donating your excess tomatoes, carrots, and other garden-grown veggies and fruits to your local food bank. This is called "Plant a Row, Grow a Row" and it is as simple as it sounds. Plant a Row, Grow a Row is a program that is supported by the Composting Council of Canada. To learn more, go to compost.org or growarow.org.

Chapter 11

Options *for* Locavores

Farming these days is variously dirty, hot, sweaty, boring, menial, messy, wet, cold, frustrating, and dirtier still. And that's when things are going well.

—Les Bowser, Canadian Farmer

How we buy our groceries has changed a lot over the last generation. Farmers' markets have exploded, for example. In Toronto, there were ten markets fifteen years ago. Now there are over sixty. I see dramatic changes much like this across the country. As well, more of us are using public community and allotment gardens to grow our own food. Why is this? I explore some of the reasons here.

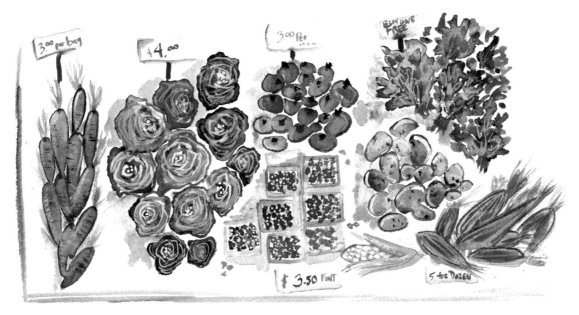

It is late summer and there are clusters of honeybees in my squash flowers, making a sound like a sanctuary full of humming monks. My vegetable garden is literally humming along this time of year, and I am delighted with its progress.

The food that we consume locally, from our own gardens and from a variety of other "local" places, has been on our radar for a few years now. The Greenbelt Farmers' Network thought that it would be useful to check in with the shoppers at some of Ontario's farmers' markets to get an understanding of why they choose to shop there and to pick up a few morsels of information along the way. As a result, they performed a survey of more than six hundred farmers' market shoppers.

Some of the conclusions are indeed illuminating. Among them were these nuggets:

- The number one reason for shopping at a farmers' market is for fresh vegetables.
- The average basket of goods is valued at $40.10.

🌿 Farmers' market shoppers are generally willing to pay a bit more for their produce, knowing that it is local and fresh.

🌿 The success of farmers' markets is "about localizing and connecting."

🌿 Frequent expressions used to describe the farmers' market experience were "food and touching" (one assumes touching the food), "fresh, tasty, local, organic," and "supporting local farmers."

MORE FAMILY MEALS

Many of those surveyed stated that their regular visits to the farmers' market impacted dramatically on their attitudes and behaviour toward mealtime at home. One in four shoppers shares more meals with family/household members than they did prior to shopping at the farmers' market. Advocates for family meals will no doubt be pleased to hear this.

Most shoppers at farmers' markets believe that they are here to stay. Their permanence is a function of the increasing popularity of accessing food via this expanding distribution channel.

LOCAL SUPERMARKETS

All of this enthusiasm for farmers' markets leads to the question, *What about the offering of "locally produced" fruit and vegetables at your local supermarket?* For some answers, I turned to one of Canada's largest independent grocers, Longo's. I contacted Michael Forgione at their head office.

In their experience, the "local food phenomena" is a growing category, and it is here to stay. "Locally produced" food ranks in the top four reasons shoppers frequent their stores. Freshness, Quality, and Overall Look and Feel also rank in the top four.

WHAT IS LOCAL?

According to Forgione, the definition of "local" at Longo's is "Ontario grown," consistent with the Foodland Ontario definition.

This is interesting. Speak to a farmer who produces for a "local" market, and you might get a different answer. Guy Farintosh of Farintosh Farms in Stouffville has his own opinion. "If you marry a local girl she is not from the other side of the province," he rightly says. "Local may not be an issue (in terms of freshness) where potatoes are concerned, but it certainly is with sweet corn, especially with the savvier locavores."

Guy raises an issue that sticks in the craw of other local farmers, I am sure. "A local farmers' market had a large sign that stated, 'Farm-Fresh Picked Corn—Picked Daily!' out on the first of July. It probably was picked daily and likely on a farm, but on the first of July that farm was likely in New Jersey. Surely this is out of the realm of 'local' produce."

Apart from being untrue, that message on the sign creates problems for legitimate producers like Farintosh. "I had a steady stream of customers in to our market in July wondering why our own corn (which is ready the first of August) is so slow."

BUYER BEWARE

Back in the aisles of the produce retailer, Michael Forgione makes it clear that the key to providing excellent quality, fresh, locally produced fruits and vegetables hinges on the relationships that the retailer has forged over the years. "The benefit of nurturing long-term relationships [with growers] literally means that we get the pick of the crop."

He goes on to say that the future of the local food movement is bright. "We believe that it will grow. Longo's is a destination for locally grown and produced foods—we feel this trend definitely has legs."

Forgione makes it clear that this retailer does not view farmers' markets or farmers who retail their product from the farm as competitors. "We feel that the Ontario Ministry of

Agriculture and Foods' Foodland Ontario program is a great example of a program that supports all food retailers."

There is a refreshingly positive note to all this talk about sourcing local food that is fresh, notwithstanding the odd vendor that is prepared to mislead the public to turn a fast buck. We can only hope that the people responsible for our farmers' markets are managing the issues that assure the consumer truth in advertising: local, fresh, organic (if that is part of the promise), and so on.

Many Canadians are now subscribing to CSAs (Community Supported Agriculture). For a fee, fresh, farm-produced food is dropped at your door direct from the farms that produce it. My son, Ben, enjoys his subscription to a local CSA. He says that the weekly surprises in the form of vegetables that he was not expecting create great opportunities to cook "outside of the box."

As we contemplate the ramifications of "buyer beware" as it relates to buying our fresh food, Michael Pollan, author of *In Defense of Food: An Eater's Manifesto*, reminds us to "shake the hand of the farmer that feeds you." Knowing your local growers can only help you by providing assurance of genuinely "local."

The bees continue to buzz in my squash blossoms, reminding me that there is a fourth option to fresh food shopping: browsing the aisles of my own vegetable garden. Life in Canada is good, especially during harvest time.

Chapter 12

the Birds *and the* Bees: *the* Talk You Never Had

Father to prepubescent son: "It is time for you and me
to talk about the birds and the bees."
Son: "Sure, Dad. What do you want to know?"

When I wrote this, Canadians were becoming aware of the decline of the honeybee population. I wanted to explain why awareness of the decline is important and what the average gardener can do about it.

Since then, I estimate that most Canadians are keenly aware of the decline of the honeybee, but most are not aware of the similar risk to our native bee population. We have over seven hundred native bee species in Canada, and many of them are more effective pollinators than the honeybee (which is a European import).

All of this is to say that while awareness is one thing, doing something about it is another.

I am impressed by many of the things that kids learn about in school today that were never talked about in my day. Subjects like multiculturalism, character, fairness, recycling, worm composting, bullying, and eliminating inappropriate remarks and behaviour toward the opposite sex are just a few. But ask a kid today about the importance of fostering honeybees in the neighbourhood, and chances are they will give you a blank stare. Come to that, most adults do not seem to understand that not only our food prosperity but also the future of civilization as we know it depends on a thriving culture of honeybees.

Albert Einstein reputedly said, "Mankind will not survive the honeybees' disappearance for more than five years." What, you might ask, did Mr. Einstein know that the rest of us don't? I wondered the same thing and did some digging for answers. What I came up with is surprising, alarming, and hopeful all at the same time.

BEES' IMPORTANCE

Bees are nature's primary pollinators. Given that many of the plants that produce our food are pollinated by bees, we would be doing ourselves a great service to pay attention to them. Seeing as reports over the last few years indicate that their population is in steep decline throughout much of the world, including where you live, nurturing and protecting them seems like a good idea.

PERFECT AND IMPERFECT FLOWERS

Many plants have "perfect" flowers, complete with both male and female sex parts. This might lead you to think that a pollinator with wings is hardly necessary. Your tomato plants, for example, do not require pollination from bees or hummingbirds or butterflies for that matter. However, any experienced gardener will tell you that the greater the population of bees in a neighbourhood the more productive the tomatoes, peppers, and potatoes (all members of the same Solanaceae family). The pollinating activity of bees is beneficial even when it is not entirely necessary.

"Imperfect" flowers exist on a host of important food plants, including all members of the cucurbit or squash family. They have female and male flowers, usually on the same plants though not always, which require a visit from one of nature's flying pollinators to mix things up. It is the transfer of pollen from flower to flower (a pollen-laden anther to stamen, to be exact) that fertilizes your pumpkin or cucumber, and nothing does it quite as efficiently as bees do. About one-third of everything that we eat has been pollinated by a bee, according to Cathy Kozma, past chair of our Toronto Beekeepers Collective.

Bees dig in to a nice squash flower looking for food and come out covered in pollen grains. I have learned that they buzz a lot when they are in the middle of the flower, in an effort to dig as deeply as possible for what they are really looking for. Buzzing is nature's way of removing the pollen and maximizing the exposure of it to the body and pollen pockets of the bee, so the theory goes. Like power-sanding a woodworking project, buzzing gets the job done more efficiently.

BEES' DECLINE

The population of bees *is* in decline. This is a fact. In many parts of Canada, we have experienced about a 30–40 per cent decline in bee population in the last ten years. In other parts of the continent the decline is much greater, especially in arid areas.

According to Cathy, the condition that is causing the decline in the bee population is referred to as CCD, or Colony Collapse Disorder. While there is no one cause for it, CCD is blamed on:

- the Varroa destructor mite
- loss of natural habitat
- monoculture agricultural practices
- widespread pesticide use

What can the average hobby gardener do to help? Considering that the average bee performs her work (and they are all female that work) within a six- and ten-kilometre radius of her home, there is lots that you can do. First, I recommend that you plant plants that are attractive and useful to bees. My list includes:

- **bachelor's buttons** (easy to grow annual)
- **borage** (useful herb and soil enhancer)
- **Russian sage** (a metre high, reliable perennial, flowers for up to eight weeks)
- **bee balm** or **Monarda** (one of my favourite perennials for the sun. Grows up to one metre.)
- **sunflowers** (kids love these.)

❧ **sage** (useful herb and rather fragrant)

❧ **oregano** (plant one and enjoy a lot. An aggressive perennial groundcover in sun.)

❧ **basil** (you want this for your tomatoes come September anyway.)

In addition, Cathy recommends that we:

❧ Plant larger patches of flowering plants to encourage bee foraging.

❧ Diversify your blooming plant portfolio. Have bee-friendly plants in bloom throughout the season.

❧ Avoid the use of pesticides.

❧ Let some of your garden naturalize. This will encourage bees to nest and tunnel without being disturbed. Note: bumblebees nest in the ground; some native bees build their nests in dead raspberry canes.

❧ Provide a constant source of water. A hive will consume about half a litre of water a day. Put out small containers of clean water and float a small piece of wood in it to provide a landing strip and access to the water.

❧ Add hollow tubes in a mason bee house around your yard.

In addition, I urge you to support your local beekeepers by buying their bee products. I can assure you that this is a labour of love, more so than a profit-seeking venture.

Chapter 13

Insect Hotels

Teaching a child not to step on a caterpillar is as valuable to the child as it is to the caterpillar.

—Bradley Millar

We still tend to think of insects as bad, much as we think of dirt as dirty. I am happy to say that things are changing for Canadians, though slowly. Read the words carefully here and note that "rot and decay" are your friends. What I attempt is to draw attention to a universe of insect activity that wants to be a part of your yard. All you have to do is invite it in.

During a recent trip to Vancouver Island, my wife and I had the pleasure of staying in a new hotel on Qualicum Beach. It was a beaut. Shortly after arriving, we went to the restaurant where we were greeted by an enthusiastic server. When we told her that we were staying in the newly minted hotel she asked abruptly, "So, how is the bed?" Mary and I looked at each other with a brief hesitation. I squeaked, "We only just arrived so we can't really say." I was pleased with myself for not saying what so swiftly ran through my mind in those brief seconds. This was not the time to be a smart aleck.

When making travel plans we often obsess over the sleeping arrangements. When I was a kid going to summer camp, the priority upon arriving was staking out a bed. And so it should come as no surprise to us that insects are not much different. Each species has their own preference for accommodations with regards to sleeping and, for that matter, breeding. (See, I read your mind there, didn't I!)

Where our yards and gardens are concerned, there has been a growing interest in biodiversity. With all the attention recently given to honeybees and their decline, gardeners are beginning to see that our activity has a dramatic impact on wildlife in our larger communities. Put another way, the birds and butterflies that you attract to your yard belong neither to you nor to your neighbour but to a bigger world of which we are only a small but impactful part. When we plant and nurture, compost and mulch, place feeders, baths, and houses for birds, we are doing much to change the biodiversity of the neighbourhood, whether we intend to or not.

My point is to suggest that you become more purposeful about these things. The arrangement that we have with Mother Nature on our real estate (whether it is terra firma or a balcony on the twelfth storey of a condo) is not one merely for our convenience but is a privilege, much like driving a car. Abuse it and severe damage can occur.

BUILD AN INSECT HOTEL

As we explore the natural world around us by planting more native plants (and we are!), why not build a hotel that attracts more insects to your garden? Let's get one thing straight: 99 per cent of the insects in your garden are beneficial. They will not seriously harm your plants and they play an important part in the dynamics that go on in the food web outside your kitchen door. Earthworms eat dirt and in digesting it produce nitrogen-rich earthworm castings that feed everything that grows in your garden. Robins eat the worms and leave free fertilizer sprinkled about your yard and garden, sometimes landing inconveniently on the deck or your head, which is supposed to be good luck.

Centipedes, beetles, millipedes, ladybugs, bumblebees, earwigs, and pill bugs all play a role in creating a garden environment rich in resources.

You can encourage insects to visit and reside at your place by building insect hotels. These can be as simple or as complex as you want to make them. There are many designs for insect hotels, and if you are a creative type, you can create your own. The key is to use natural materials and to arrange it in such a manner that insects will find it attractive enough to move in. This is where the fastidious among us have trouble with the concept, as the truth is that insects do not like a sanitized environment, like the one they advertise on the plastic, hermetically sealed drinking glasses you find at the Holiday Inn. Insects like messy. They thrive on clods of rotting leaves, rough-cut lumber, or better still, a stack of split firewood. Preferences vary from species to species, but you get the idea.

Mason bees, which are not inclined to sting and are more efficient pollinators than the much-ballyhooed honeybee, breed in holes six to nineteen millimetres in diameter, and at least fourteen centimetres long. Dead wood in various stages of decomposition and woody debris attract beetles, wood-boring insects, centipedes, and millipedes—providing the wood remains a little moist.

House bricks make a great foundation for an insect hotel. The holes in them provide spaces for amphibians like frogs and toads. To maximize their population in your yard, position your hotel near a water feature.

Longer, open-ended tunnels make great homes for snakes. Despite all the bad press that they receive, snakes are a good thing for the garden as they eat rodents and a whole host of invasive insects. They are an important link in the food web.

If you build a layered or multi-storied hotel, plan for a few tunnels that lead to segregated, open, grass-free areas beneath it. Toads and snakes burrow beneath the soil to overwinter and hibernate and have an easier time of it when the earth is exposed.

Fallen leaves, layers of bark, and plant debris act like a forest floor and tend to hold moisture, providing habitat for many kinds of beneficial beetles. Twigs provide a home for beneficial ladybugs.

WHERE TO BUILD

Build your insect hotel in semi-shade, using the side exposed to sunshine for the bee residence and the darker, shaded side for cool-loving amphibians like garden toads and salamanders. Don't plan on moving your insect hotel for a long while as insects have trouble reorienting to a new home. This explains why it may take a few years for new residents to set up shop in your creation.

As for maintenance, relax. There is little that you need to do. If you are attracting mason bees using cardboard tubes, you will need to replace them every spring. Don't panic if you see fungi and moss growing on your insect hotel, and there is a good chance that you will end up with mushrooms growing on the damp, shady side. This is all good.

If you find that birds are enjoying a meal at your insect hotel, secure hardware cloth or chicken wire at least two centimetres out from the surface of the insect buffet. This will give the poor dears a fighting chance at reproducing while the birds find another source to forage.

And finally, the hardest part of this exercise: relax. Learn to leave natural debris where it falls in your garden. Remember that rot and decay are your friends.

Come autumn, rake the leaves off your lawn and on to your garden soil, where they will eventually break down and provide habitat for insects and small animals in the meantime.

If you are reading this and wondering, what on Earth is the world coming to? My answer is this: the natural world is coming to you by way of a new generation and new thinking about what a beautiful garden really is.

It is time to welcome Mother Nature home.

Chapter 14

What Gardeners Can Learn *from* Farmers

Farming is a profession of hope.

—Brian Brett, Canadian writer

J ust as we can learn from nature by beeing (see how I did that?) sensitive to her cues for various garden activities, we can also learn from farmers. Many of them have been tilling the soil longer than we have, and they tend to take growing plants seriously as they rely on them to make a living.

I remember the first words written by Dr. Spock in his landmark book on raising children, "Follow your instincts." In other words, we are naturally armed to do the right thing, when our intentions are honourable. And what could be more honourable than sowing, planting, and growing—in other words, nurturing?

I have a great deal of respect for the farming community. They appreciate the value of soil and the seeds that germinate in it perhaps more than any other profession in the world. They generally know what works and what doesn't. And they have learned to take their own cues from nature: to work with her rather than fight against her.

❧

If there is one group of people who watch spring approach with the same anticipation as gardeners, it is farmers. Like gardeners, they are land stewards and plant aficionados. Unlike most gardeners, farmers depend on their land stewardship and plant knowledge to cultivate their livelihoods (versus doing it for fun). There is a great deal that gardeners can learn from farmers, both scientific knowledge which has been developed in our universities and agricultural extension programs, and cultural knowledge, which has been passed down for generations from one farmer to the next.

Here are the top four lessons that we have learned from farmers:

1. Crop Rotation

The practice of rotating crops benefits farmers by breaking insect and disease cycles, allowing deeper rooted crops to improve soil structure for plants with less root vigor, as well as by adding nutrients to the soil and increasing the content of organic matter. Annual crop rotation around a field contributes to more reliable crops, healthier harvests, and a better bottom line.

One crop which is particularly dependent on a proper rotation in the garden is tomatoes, which should be moved every year. Tomatoes are particularly susceptible to soil-borne diseases such as verticillium wilt and early blight. Moving them also helps avoid soil-borne pests such as wireworms and beetle larvae. I recommend a three-year rotation where year two incorporates a "Cabbage Crop" (such as broccoli, Brussels sprouts, cabbage, cauliflower, kohlrabi, or kale), and year three an onion crop (such as garlic, leeks, onions, scallions, shallots).

For container gardeners who want to plant year after year, I recommend that you remove and replace your soil each spring, making sure to clean the container to rid it of pathogens. I do this with all of my containers regardless of what I am growing.

2. Reduced Tillage or No-Till

In an agricultural setting, excessive tillage (i.e., plowing or cultivating) destroys soil structure, which plants depend on to grow and store nutrients. It also leads to soil compaction and erosion while accelerating the decomposition of soil's organic matter.

Soil structure and organic matter should concern all gardeners. "No-till" gardening generally requires that after the bed is established, the surface is never disturbed. To retain the highest degree of natural soil-borne nutrients, mulch soil to prevent drying out and crusting over.

When you plant, pull the mulch back and disturb the soil only to plant into the ground. Leaves, compost, finely ground bark mulch, and straw all make great mulches.

Leaves should be spread no more than twenty-five centimetres thick when dry or four centimetres thick when matted and wet. Come July, all those leaves will have decomposed and been taken down into the topsoil by earthworms, where the material is converted into nitrogen-rich worm castings. If you don't have lots of worm activity in your soil, you can buy worm castings by the bag at your garden retailer. I mix them one part to ten parts soil.

Natural nutrients are added to the soil as the mulch breaks down. Your earthworm population will explode. And you will experience a dramatic decrease in water requirements.

3. Feed the Soil

With each harvest of nutritious crops leaving the field, farmers know that the nutrient value removed when the plant is harvested needs to go back into the soil. These nutrients are fed back into the soil as compost, well-rotted manure, or fertilizers where they are available to the next crop. And the cycle continues.

The nutrient cycle in the garden is really no different, so to expect the garden to absorb nutrients without first feeding the soil is misguided. By far the best thing you can do for your garden is to start a compost pile, diverting kitchen waste from landfills and adding rich nutrients and organic matter back into your soil. When I run out of compost from my own pile, I supplement with BioMax, the only brand of manure approved by the Composting Council of Canada; it is also Organic Materials Review Institute (OMRI) certified.

4. Pollinators Do the Heavy Lifting

Generally farmers are paying close attention to the state of our bees and pollinator populations, as one-third of all our food is directly pollinated by insects and birds.

Gardeners can do their part to protect pollinating insect populations by creating a habitat for them. Design a garden that incorporates tall, native grasses and pollinator-friendly perennials such as blanket flower, Black-eyed Susan, bee balm, coreopsis, mint and purple prairie clover (all of which can be planted in spring, before the summer heat "hits home" for next year's blossom). Not only will this type of garden look stunning and support a range of pollinators, it will also be less susceptible to disease and less vulnerable to drought.

Gardeners have the luxury of pursuing our labour of love free from many of the pressures which farmers face, mostly because we are not making a living at our pastime. Through our shared experience, we can learn from one another to maximize our productivity, satisfaction, and environmental contributions in the garden.

Chapter 15

You Have *a* Notification *from* Mother Nature

MARK AND BEN CULLEN

Science has never drummed up quite as effective a tranquilizing agent as a sunny spring day.

—W. Earl Hall (1897–1969)

While this story will not rock your world (unlike other content in this book) it serves as a reminder that Nature is here to show us the way.

How easy it is to forget that the natural cycle of life in your yard and in your neighbourhood parks can serve as reminders to engage in the gardening experience. Here is some practical information that will help get you started.

Early each spring gardeners get ready to storm the seed racks with their planting schedule in hand. We have seen some gardeners who were so organized they could feed their plans into a computer and let a robot do the work for them! The tricky part is, sometimes Mother Nature has other plans. As both an art and science, gardening requires an organized approach which can be adapted to the unforeseen, especially where weather is concerned. As farmers say, "Want to make Mother Nature laugh? Show her your plans."

One way to approach your veggie planting schedule is to consider Mother Nature's signals. The scientific name for this approach is phenology: "the study of cyclic and seasonal natural phenomena, especially in relation to climate and plant and animal life." Simply put, it is a process where the gardener uses cues that are sent from nature to attend to certain gardening tasks.

Phenology is especially useful when trying to decide what and when to plant in the vegetable garden. Below are our phenology tips and how to interpret them.

🌱 **When the crocuses bloom and maple trees start to flower,** the soil temperature is around five degrees Celsius, which means you are ready to plant **spinach, kale, Swiss chard, lettuce, bok choy, parsnips, peas, and radishes,** as these crops all require eighty to one hundred days to mature. Lettuce is the exception (sixty days), which should be planted biweekly throughout the season up to midsummer to keep the production coming right into the late fall. Look for mesclun mix, Tango green leaf lettuce, and Lollo Rossa red leaf lettuce. Remember, when you are harvesting Swiss chard and kale, you should pick the lower leaves as the plant matures.

🌱 **When the dandelions bloom** the soil temperature is around ten degrees Celsius, and perfect for planting **Chinese cabbage, leeks, onions, and turnips.** Leeks are fun because they germinate easily, love the sun, and are low maintenance. Generally, leeks are insect- and disease-free. You can harvest them late in the season when everything else has finished. As they mature throughout the summer, mound up the soil around them twelve to fifteen centimetres high (we do this while weeding) to give them their white/cream colour and sweet flavour. Mark's favourite variety is Lancelot.

🌱 **When full-sized daffodils start blooming** (not the small flowering jonquils) the soil temperature is around fifteen degrees Celsius, which means you are ready to plant **beans, beets, and brassicas.** Brassicas include a whole bunch of great veggie crops including broccoli, cabbage, kale, rutabaga, and turnip. For beans, try Provider or Dusky Green for green beans on a small and productive bush. Yellow beans that we like are Gold Rush and Gold Mine. For something different, try Blue Hyacinth beans. This vine-type bean will grow vertically up almost anything and is a very striking blue-purple. The fruit comes late in the season. Grow for the ornamental quality; it is really quite stunning. The beans themselves can be mildly poisonous, so don't confuse them with the edible types.

🌱 **When the bearded iris and lilacs start blooming,** the soil temperature is around twenty degrees Celsius, which means you are ready to plant the warmest season crops such as **tomatoes, peppers, cucumbers, and eggplant.** These will be transplants which were started indoors eight weeks prior or bought at a retailer. Tomatoes are the favourite homegrown Canadian crop. Mark grows over two hundred plants and about twenty different varieties. Look for Big Beef (All American Award winner), Sweet Heart (grape type), Sweet One Million (super sweet cherry type), and Early Girl (earliest ripening). Brandywine is a popular heirloom/heritage type but the blight can get it early in a wet season, as it often does the heritage varieties.

Peppers belong in the hottest part of your garden, as they love the sun. Mark grows sweet types such as California Green, a stalwart, Early Sensation for earlier fruit, and Fat n' Sassy for huge, late-season fruit. Ben likes the hot peppers and recommends Hungarian Hot Wax, Cayenetta (All American Selections winner), Cheyenne (hot cherry type), and Chicken Itza. Remember that tomatoes and peppers are heavy feeders, so make sure to add generous amounts of compost when planting and fertilize with an organic fertilizer if necessary.

❧ **When oak leaves are the size of a squirrel's ear,** it is time to plant **corn and virtually all other hot crops: melons, pumpkins, gourds,** or any crop that thrives in the heat and wilts in cool temperatures can be planted at this time. In my zone 5 garden, this is usually the first week of June.

Naturally, there is a degree of good judgement which should accompany nature's signals to get out in the garden. Sometimes there is no substitute for common sense, which is why we watch the weather forecast carefully each planting season. Take cues from Mother Nature as reminders of what to plant when, and enjoy the fact that a daffodil blooming is nature's reminder that you can put your bean seeds in the ground. Sure beats the notifications that vibrate on our cellphones.

Part III

The VALUE of the GARDENING EXPERIENCE

As I wrote these essays, with some help from son Ben, I was moved outside of my box or "comfort zone" and encouraged to see my world differently. In my view, I spend way too much time banking. Putting money in and taking it out (paying bills). The consistent coming and going of cash wears me down and gives me no pleasure. My gardening experience, however, gives me infinitely more pleasure. There is simply no competition on the fulfillment scale between banking and gardening.

Banking has much in common with buying insurance, writing a will, buying gas (buying most anything), lining up to get loaded onto a plane (lining up for most anything), television commercials during my favourite hockey games (interruptions to my fun time), and some days wading through seemingly infinite numbers of email messages, sorting the good ones from the useless.

This is not a gripe, just an acknowledgement that much of a typical day is simply the grind of life. We do a lot of stuff because we must do it.

Not so gardening. I remind my retail friends at Home Hardware (and any other retailers that will listen) that our customers in the Lawn and Garden department are spending discretionary dollars. It is not like they are fixing their leaky toilet. When a customer wades into our section of the store they are looking for some pleasure, a payback for the trouble of fixing the toilet (or banking).

There are over 200,000 Canadians employed in the horticultural business. There are more than $14 billion generated through it. And almost all that money is spent willingly by the consumer in search of…well, that is the question, isn't it! What is it that we are in search of in the garden?

Are we attempting to enhance our lives by making them brighter and greener? Or are we just keeping up with the Joneses? I believe in the former. And as I wrote this part of *Escape to Reality*, I came to believe it even more. Here, we dig deep in an effort to understand what motivates us to spend time in the garden. Much more to the point, we gain a deeper understanding of how we can make the time and experience in the garden more meaningful to us.

The garden experience sets me free. I hope that the essays in this part help you feel more free while out there, too.

Chapter 16

Dear Garden, I Have Changed

*Changing and actually improving
are two quite different skills.*

—Dr. SunWolf, 2015 tweet

I am a cancer survivor.

In 2013, my GP discovered a spike in my PSA (prostate-specific antigen) blood readings.

He sent me to an urologist. "I could be wasting your time. But my only job is to help keep you healthy." So off I went.

The story that follows was inspired by my experience under the knife and in recovery. I struggled with the idea that my experience could help others and maybe save a life or two. And the short answer is: men, get your PSA test annually and look for movement in the number, not just the number itself.

But what was the connection between my health challenge and my gardening experience?

Read on for the answer.

⁖

Last year on New Year's, I wrote a column titled, "Dear Garden: I Will Change." It generated more comments and interest from readers than any of my other articles. I pulled it from my files to stimulate some thought on how, in fact, I had changed and why. I hope that this written reflection is as helpful to you as it was for me.

I WILL LISTEN MORE

In January 2013, I wrote: "My world is full of noise. Emails fill my head with information and planned responses. This year I am going to be more attentive to birdsong, wind in the trees, and the buzz of a honeybee visiting a nearby flower. I will take more time to absorb the music of nature precisely where I find it. I will turn off my cellphone. I will leave the power equipment in the shed whenever possible."

I changed all right. Perhaps without making a conscious attempt at listening more, it happened anyway. As the soil warmed and the month of April slipped over the horizon, May gave rise to more than fourteen thousand daffodils that I had planted on my property over the past seven years.

On May 4, I attended a long-awaited appointment with a urologist. My GP had sent me to get my prostate checked out as the results of recent PSA tests indicated that there may be a problem. During my brief first visit with the specialist it was determined that more tests were recommended, which I undertook.

By mid-May, I had received the news that, indeed, I had prostate cancer. It was serious enough that I needed to give it immediate attention, though it was not life-threatening.

The day the doctor gave me the bad news I drove slowly, in search of some green space. I found a small park, located under a hydro right-of-way with one large tree growing on the margin of the parking lot. I sat on the cool green grass, looked at the tree, and began asking questions.

When I arrived home, I sat on the front porch and watched the feathered wildlife while I continued to ask questions, this time directing them to no one in particular. But the big oak tree in our front yard seemed to be listening.

I WILL OBSERVE MORE

Last year I wrote: "There was the tiniest of bird nests in one of my dwarf apple trees this past summer. I only noticed it when I drove past it on the ride-on lawn mower and it brushed against my shoulder. It belonged to a finch mother-in-waiting who was more than attentive. She was a saint for sitting on her eggs, five of them smaller than my pinkie fingernail. All bird mothers are saints. Next year, I will get off the ride-on mower and spend more time wandering through my apple orchard without any specific purpose, other than just doing it."

Well, I did walk through that orchard a lot more this year. For one, the trees grew a prodigious quantity of red, ripe apples that required my attention. When I was not picking them I was watching for the return of mother finch, with no luck.

I WILL CREATE MORE

Last year I wrote: "One of the wonders of humankind is our ability to dream and convert dreams into something real. Gardens are the result of this ability. There is, after all, no animal that dreams and creates quite like we do. This ability can destroy nature or build it up."

On June 13, I was admitted to Toronto East General Hospital to undergo a radical prostatectomy. Two days later I was released. The excellent staff there handed me off to my excellent wife who took me home for the six-week recovery. This journey, I was to discover, was just beginning.

As my body took its own sweet time healing, I was instructed to not push a lawn mower, dig any holes, or swing a golf club until I had the "all-clear" from my surgeon. My next appointment with him was six weeks away. I spent a lot more time on that front porch, watching for hummingbirds, changes in the weather, visitors pulling into the driveway, and imagining an amazing golf swing. The birds and visitors came and—for six weeks—my golf game never looked so good, proving once again that I have an active fantasy life.

And dream I did. I conjured up images of colour and cool shade: an enhanced yard and garden, without the competition of twitch grass or Canada thistles. I imagined a new plan for my acre of vegetables and a green roof over my woodshed. I discovered that when you sit and think long enough you can come up with all kinds of make-work projects.

I WILL FEED AND NURTURE MORE

Last year I wrote: "If there is just one thing that I have learned from my garden over the years it is this: one reaps what one sows. I feed the soil and the soil gives back aplenty. My vegetable garden is the greatest gauge of this, though the exercise is equally informing with my ornamental trees and perennials. By exercise, I mean the annual practice of adding a large quantity of natural, organic material to the soil in an effort to build up the community of insects, beneficial bacteria, and mycorrhizae that make up the foundation of the plants that grow there."

I put my money where my mouth was on this one. I spread almost forty cubic metres of mushroom compost/sand mix over my garden (with some help from my friend Rudy, as I had to convalesce). My soil supplier was delighted. My garden has never looked better.

I WILL SHARE MORE

I wrote: "This New Year's I am taking the time to look around me. Who can benefit from my garden? As my vegetable garden grows and matures throughout the season I bring the excess produce to my buddy Ted at his local deli for him to sell. I don't charge him for it. He sells some of it right off of the shelf and makes his famous pesto sauce and soup with the remainder, which he also sells to his fortunate clientele. The money is turned over to the local food bank."

So I did and Ted did, too. There was a record crop of tomatoes this year in my garden, perhaps the result of all that hopefulness and praying for a successful recovery spilled over into their roots.

Recover I have. In late July 2013, my urologist told me that I am cancer free and could move on to the monitoring stage of the plan.

Yes, I changed all right. Not in ways that I had predicted a year ago, nor for reasons that I anticipated. But I have changed. Through the miracle of nature's healing and modern science I am a new man, for better or worse. I am one of the lucky ones. I guess it us up to me to determine which outcome will evolve: the better or the worse.

I look forward to my new garden year with great anticipation and renewed energy. It is up to us to get our knees dirty and feel good about it. To experience gardening in a fuller way. For the men reading this, get your PSA checked annually by a doctor that you trust. Then, perhaps, all of us will have made progress this coming year.

Chapter 17

What Your Garden Means *to* You

Dreams are today's answers
to tomorrow's questions.

—Edgar Cayce (1877–1945)

When Brenda, my assistant, came up with the idea of asking my Facebook followers to share their answer to the question, *What does your garden mean to you?* I had no idea how profoundly people really felt. The content was too good to just let hang out there in cyberspace. I had to share it in print. I hope you enjoy it as much as I did.

More than fifty people expressed their thoughts. Many were quite personal. As I review these responses, they prompt reflection on the meaning that my own gardening experience has to me.

Some readers responded with reflections on their earliest experiences in the garden.

Linda answered: "My garden is a tribute to my grandparents. One of my earliest memories is how proud I was when my maternal grandmother allowed me to go into the garden and pick a cucumber.... I remember my grandfather, well into hi eighties, hoeing his garden and telling my dad to collect all of the cow patties to make compost tea. Both my grandparents have been gone more than thirty years but every time I am in the garden I think of them."

Edna replied: "My love for gardening began when my godmother gave me a dozen gladiolus bulbs for my eleventh birthday....Our thirty-year-old garden has changed so many times and it gives us such pleasure."

Heather offered: "Over the years I have come to love the recharging effect of working outside in the quiet and enjoy the different elements carefully chosen to remind me of the inspiring gardeners in my life, my mom and my grandmothers. It is a labour of love."

Others opened up and shared some very personal feelings and experiences.

Pam wrote: "My garden means healing as I started to really work and create it when my eldest son died. I started a memory garden for him. Each year I planted something that reminded me of him."

Nancy answered: "My garden is my lifeline. Even after working all day at my job it is so wonderful to come home and be able to spend time in my garden.... Getting dirty, birdsong, wildlife, all remind me that I am truly part of this Earth."

Gail said: "My garden brings peace and happiness."

Judy replied: "My garden is a true sanctuary. It breathes new life into me. I laugh there, cry there, I visit there and the best part is I can share it. As a single mom for many years my garden became cheap therapy for me. It was reliable, always there for me, any time of the day."

Vicky contributed: "Peace and reflection."

Cathy wrote: "My garden takes me to a very quiet place, my place. To watch every plant grow amazes me. Nature at its best is all around me."

Janice: "The garden is a place where I can commune with the dirt and stay in the moment."

Others talked about food and its connection to gardening.

Linda said: "Fresh produce for me and my family, and preserves for later eating: sharing of flowers to those who appreciate the gesture."

Carrie replied: "My garden, especially my vegetable garden, gives me a sense of accomplishment."

Parents and grandparents emphasized the connection between gardening and kids.

Tracy offered: "[My garden] is a way to teach my three young daughters about nature and nurture and true beauty."

Julie wrote: "Any time I am in my garden is the only normal thing in my life!"

I love it when readers talk to me like they talk to their husbands.

Lesleigh said: "Well, Mark, I will tell you what I tell my husband when he posed the questions, 'You spend how much on the garden?' Flowers make me happy. I actually hated having a

garden as a child. Until it came time to turn the cucumbers into pickles…. I actually go home on my lunch break to garden. It resets me. I find weeding therapeutic. But above all, the most meaningful thing about gardening is the traditional values that go with it."

Louis Armstrong sang it first, about those green trees and red roses, too. You know the song.

Laura offered: "My garden allows me to believe there is good in this world. I see birds, butterflies, wasps, bees, moths, and hummingbirds all happy! This gives me hope that the world will one day hum and be happy."

Sharon wrote: "My garden is an absolute wonder. Along with a glass of wine [of course], weeding, tilling, wandering and pondering…all a total joy."

There is something poetic about that weeding, tilling, wandering, and pondering. Thanks, Sharon! And thanks to all those who responded so meaningfully.

My dear friend, the late Hugh Beaty, used to reply to every story with this word, which I love, and Linda used it, too: "Wonderful!"

And finally, a poem worthy of a new garden season that I share with the author's permission. Linda wrote:

The spiders. The weeds. The bird stole my seeds.
My aching sore back.
My pebble-marked knees.
A vine with a choke-hold.
A flowerpot crack.
A kinked garden hose.
Oh! The neighbourhood cat.
But the colours. The shapes.

The smells. The sights.
Nothing compares to those flowering delights.
As I sit on my swing and sip my tea.
I laugh and giggle with glee.
Sleep well, my garden, but promise one thing.
You will come back to visit next spring.

Amen!

You can follow Mark and Ben on Facebook at MarkCullenGardening.

Chapter 18

a Home, a Job, and a Friend

I want to be thoroughly used up when I die,
for the harder I work the more I live.
—George Bernard Shaw (1856–1950)

You can interpret this story about social enterprise one of two ways: providing meaningful work for people has its own merits, or working with plants while earning a living has therapeutic benefits. Or possibly both hold true.

My late mother said to me once, "You know, it is interesting, raising five kids. You are forever coaching and teaching and then one day you wake up and realize that your kids are teaching you."

I had such a moment the day that Maggie Griffin invited me to coach and advise her management team. Since I wrote this story, Maggie has retired as president of Parkdale Green Thumb Enterprises. Angel Beyde, who has taken the reins, continues to invite me to advisory meetings for their company. And I continue to learn.

❦

As I strolled into the boardroom early in the morning, a stranger to this place and its people, I had no idea that the person who sat across from me had been living with serious challenges for many years. Mental illness is like that.

Outwardly, there are often no signs of the struggles in one's past. The evidence of a history of health challenges lies buried. The symptoms are often clear enough: homelessness, joblessness, and sometimes an inability to get up in the morning or to face another human.

All I knew for sure was that I had been asked to join a meeting of professional gardeners, people who tend plants for a living, and that at some point in their past, most of them were unemployed but now worked in a for-profit company that was born in the world of social enterprise.

I know something about running a business, as I have been doing it for a few decades. But "social enterprise" was new to me. Since then, one of the clearest definitions of social enterprise that I've seen, which comes from the BC Centre for Social Enterprise, is that it has two goals: to achieve social, cultural, community economic and/or environmental outcomes and to earn revenue. Sometimes the business is supported by a not-for-profit funding partner like the United Way. It was the good people at United Way Toronto who first introduced me to the idea a couple of years ago. As I learned more about the concept, I offered the benefit of my business experience to them, and they asked me to meet ad-hoc with Parkdale Green Thumb Enterprises, a landscape maintenance company in the west end of the city.

Maggie Griffin was responsible for running Parkdale Green Thumb for thirteen years. While she manages a business and has the usual challenges of dealing with suppliers, customer relations, and government interventions, she also employs a team of people who otherwise face barriers to employment. The success of Maggie's business is two-fold: as a business that provides services and generates cash flow, and as a means to provide opportunity for people who might otherwise not have access to employment.

The Toronto Enterprise Fund (TEF) annual report for December 2016 reads, "The Toronto Social Enterprise fund finances enterprises that connect people facing employment barriers with job training and work opportunities. Since its inception in 2000, TEF has funded 45 social enterprises, which have collectively employed and/or trained over 2,500 people. Currently, we provide operating grants to a portfolio of 15 enterprises and seed funding to two."

❧

I like Parkdale Green Thumb for a few reasons. First, social enterprise just makes sense. As Maggie has said, "What people really want is a home, a job and a friend." Working in an environment that respects your humanity can provide dignity in the hardscrabble, competitive world of "business as usual."

Secondly, Parkdale Green Thumb engages people in paid positions where they can experience the miracle of the healing power of plants while on payroll. As one employee remarked, "The social purpose aspect of Parkdale Green Thumbs gave me the courage to apply for the job. Starting back to work was the single greatest leap forward toward living a full life again. I was exercising, socializing and feeling productive. With each day I gained more confidence. This has led to other employment, new friends and a plan for the future."

Today, Parkdale Green Thumb specializes in the installation and maintenance of plantings in business improvement areas around the west-centre core of the city. They do not own cars for transportation, so employees travel by public transit. Last year they spent just over $6,000 on fares to get their people around to various jobs. Knowing how much it costs to run a car for a year, this sounds like a worthwhile investment to me.

Should you be sitting on a streetcar someday when a couple of people wander onto the car with hedge shears and a watering can in hand, you just might be witness to the Parkdale Green Thumb's work in progress.

In the first couple of years, Maggie explains, many customers made their decision to hire Parkdale Green Thumb on account of their social infrastructure: they wanted to support otherwise jobless people. But, over time, customers have turned over their landscape maintenance work to the group on account of its ability to compete in a crowded business environment.

The truth is no one who works in social enterprise is looking for a handout. That is, to a very large extent, the point of it all. People who are otherwise marginalized in our society get up in the morning knowing that they can make a valuable contribution just like anyone else meeting the demands of paid work. This social enterprise, I have learned, is basically about creating opportunities for people who could not enter the world of productive work. The benefits extend far beyond those of earning a paycheque.

When I asked her how her experience with Parkdale Green Thumb has changed her life, Maggie responds, "As I reflect on my years with Green Thumbs I understand the power of the possibility of the broader community and our somewhat marginalized community working together and discarding old labels. We become defined by abilities rather than disabilities. As an employee rather than being defined by mental health and labelled that way.

I now have a greater understanding of how a community can enrich marginal people's lives."

And finally, last word to the employee who did not wish to be named: "I can't express the gratitude I feel for the part Green Thumbs has played in giving me my life back."

While I was asked to share my experience and "expertise" with Maggie and her team, I realize now how much I learned in just one meeting. And how much more I must learn.

In recent years, I have had the privilege of sitting on the selection committee for Social Enterprise annual funding grants. Through United Way of Greater Toronto we have funded a wide variety of businesses: a contracting company that installs low-flow toilets in public housing, a tea shop managed and staffed by those with hearing impairment, and a craft workshop staffed by people living with AIDS, to name just three.

Each time I attend the panel I learn a lot about the world of social enterprise and the important need that it helps to meet in our communities.

Chapter 19

Promise Me a Rose Garden

I only went out for a walk and finally concluded to
stay out till sundown, for going out, I found,
was really going in.

—John Muir (1838–1914)

I n this story, I explore a new measure of wealth. Not the one that your investment advisor talks so earnestly about, but the wealth that comes from experiences outside of our usual boxes. Like your home, office, or even the hockey arena. "Out there" in the garden or local park we are exposed to sunshine, wind, the sounds of songbirds, and, on a good day, the smell of damp soil.

We become better people for it. And wealthier.

I have only been hospitalized once in my adult life. I spent a couple of days in Toronto East General (now the Michael Garron Hospital) several years ago, recovering from radical prostate surgery. It was the first time as an adult that I had the experience of hospitalization and I understand now why so many people just want to go home. Perhaps, with a measure of luck, there are windows at home.

There was a window in my hospital room. It looked out over a bank of air conditioners that whirred on end, and if I looked over the horizon of the HVAC units I could see a street lined with trees. There was one tree that stood out for me, not for any reason except that it was big enough for me to see well from a distance. It's dominance on the horizon impressed me and I focused on it as I struggled with the pain of a substantial incision. I would look at that tree and reflect on the time I would spend appreciating trees more deeply when I was released.

PLANTS EQUAL SHORTER HOSPITAL STAYS

It turns out that I am not unique in this regard. In the early 1980s, a researcher visited a hospital in Pennsylvania and gathered information about patients who had undergone gallbladder surgery. In those days, a gallbladder patient would need a week to two weeks' recovery in the hospital. According to Adam Alter, the hospital had views of a brick wall on one side and on the other, a view of a stand of trees. Other than that, the rooms were identical. "How did patients recover, relative to their physical location?" researchers asked.

You are likely way ahead of me on this and already have guessed that the view of the trees produced positive results. Those who looked out on to the brick wall needed, on average, a full day more to recover.

Consider the math on this and let us assume that each of the patients stayed for a full two weeks. The "brick wall patients" stayed for one extra day: fourteen days versus fifteen amounts to a 7 per cent longer stay. The study goes on to reveal that, by some measures, patients who gazed out at a natural scene were four times better off than those who faced a wall.

Since this study took place at Paoli Memorial Hospital, myriad other studies have proven the same basic principle: we *need* nature. She heals us and helps us to focus.

KIDS AND PLANTS

Where kids are concerned, a whole new genre of study and thinking has emerged that supports the concept of "free-range kids." If you visit the website by the same name (freerangekids.com), you will discover a whole new world to bring up your kids or grandkids. The contributor, Lenore Skenazy, believes that kids are safer and smarter than our culture gives them credit for. In her business as a "super nanny" she advises parents on her innovative methods of child rearing.

In a recent post on Skenazy's website, a Georgia mom posted that three police officers knocked on her door. A neighbour had reported that a four-and-a-half-year-old was playing in the park behind her house—a park that is an extension of her backyard. "We bought our home *for* the backyard and access to the park," exclaimed Kim, the blogging mom. The person who made the call, legitimately concerned for the safety and well-being of the child, accused the mom of being negligent.

The question that begs asking is, "What point is best to let kids explore nature unfettered by adult intervention?" I, for one, do not have the answer. But I do know that kids need the experience of discovering the wonders that only nature can bring. I am not advocating for irresponsible parenting. I am merely pointing out that there are benefits to letting kids explore the world outside of four walls and away from computers and without limiting interventions by adults.

FOREST BATHING

When I am old and unable to get places under my own power, I hope that someone will wheel me down to the front door of the seniors' home to catch a bus to a nearby forest. The Japanese have been doing this for generations and it is a growing trend today. *Shinrin-yoku*, or forest bathing, requires patients to walk or just sit in a densely wooded forest for extended periods of time. Compared to people who walk through urban areas, forest bathers experience lower blood pressure, lower pulse rates, and lower cortisol levels, a marker for reduced stress.

Experiences with Mother Nature do not provide the *perfect* upbringing for kids, a process for our own aging, or for patients' hospital recovery periods. But she sure can help!

Chapter 20
Health Benefits
of Nature

The greatest wealth is health.

—Virgil (70 BC–19 BC)

If there is one facility in each Canadian municipality that fosters stress, it likely is the local hospital. After all, it is when we experience both physical and mental stress that we seek services there.

To truly prosper, we must learn how to de-stress the typical hospital experience. Here is an idea worth considering: green up the surroundings.

I have some fascinating news for the federal minister of health and every provincial premier and health minister across the country. There is a way to reduce the growing reliance on our health-care system by helping people who are in a hospital heal faster and reducing their medication during a hospital stay: healthy landscapes.

While attending a recent public event at Sunnybrook Health Sciences Centre, environmental services expert Rohan Harrison handed me a booklet titled "The Link Between Landscapes & Health." This little tome provides evidence that healthy landscapes around our hospitals help in a measurable way to reduce hospital stays. The impact of a healthy tree canopy, colourful gardens, and lush green landscapes on human health has long been known but not well quantified, until now.

I've summarized below what I learned from reading this invaluable booklet.

"I WANT TO GO HOME."

Studies have found that exposure to healthy landscapes benefits hospitalized patients with improved sleep, better pain management, and a reduction in post-operative stays.

Just think about this for a minute: when we plant trees and "nurture nature" on the property that surrounds a hospital, we reduce costs by moving patients out more quickly.

As a recent client (I had a radical prostatectomy a few years ago), I can tell you that getting out of the hospital was *my* number one priority on that occasion. There is even today a snapshot of a particular tree that I could see outside my window.

Sunnybrook makes it clear in their booklet that "supporting the practice that healthy landscapes are not about warfare against pests, but rather the welfare of plants (and patients, by extension). Properly resourced plants are healthy and more able to protect themselves in a pesticide-free environment."

REDUCE DEPRESSION

Healthy landscapes provide positive benefits for people suffering from major depressive disorders and enhance psychological well-being within minutes of exposure.

Imagine that you are feeling stressed about something. Anxiety is taking control and you need a release. You are led outside to a green, oxygen-rich environment where you can breathe deeply. The result? A lessening of the burden.

Not long ago these "green spaces" were reserved for smokers. I believe that many hospitals have changed that policy, and now these environmentally rich areas are accessible to all patients, smoke-free.

CLEANER AIR

Green spaces enhance overall air quality, as pollution and dust can deplete oxygen from the air we breathe. Without sufficient oxygen, our bodies can experience exhaustion, fatigue, depression, muscle aches, respiratory difficulty, and memory problems. A lawn area of a mere 250 square metres provides enough oxygen for a family of four to breathe daily.

I am a "defender of the lawn" and was very glad to read this. When we replace lawns with asphalt or paving stone we are indeed going backwards as a society.

ENCOURAGE ACTIVITY

Taking advantage of the outdoor environment often encourages physical activity, which is critical to maintaining a healthy body weight throughout life. Encouraging outdoor activity can help address this common goal.

By "activity," booklet authors, Sunnybrook Environmental Services, could mean most anything, even a shuffle to a park bench while leaning on a walker is better than sitting in the crowded hallway watching the world go by. There is cleaner air in the green space, a more benign environment where birds sing, wind blows, and clouds move passively through the sky.

In our busy, bustling lives we often forget the therapeutic effects of being surrounded by nature. We even forget that we are part of it, products of a natural system through which we were conceived and grow into adults. A chance to escape the sterile environment of a hospital can be viewed as an opportunity, indeed.

DIVERSITY PROVIDES ITS OWN MAGIC

This is what Sunnybrook call their "multi-storey" approach to planting. The selection of a wide variety of plant materials, each with their own list of benefits, encourages the promotion of beneficial organisms. "When diverse species are planted, garden plants are better able to withstand attacks from both insects and disease."

It helps that they produce their own compost from dead plant material, mulch garden beds, and trees with natural, recycled material to minimize weeds and watering. They avoid the use of chemical pesticides and do whatever they can to promote "biodiversity that supports sustainability."

If you have spent any time at Sunnybrook you know that all of this is true. Also true is the fact that government can save a lot of money by encouraging and investing in healthy landscapes around hospitals and other health facilities.

Chapter 21
Observing Beauty

Wouldn't it be an exhilarating tonic for the soul to take
a moment to appreciate the simple, good things in life
which are so bountiful...?

—Author unknown, c. 1949

I wrote this mid-winter, and you can tell. I am in a reflective mood and trying to imagine what it is like to be in the garden, not doing anything in particular, just the sensation of being.

Not all gardeners are created equal. My late father would have called me a plantsman. My interest in gardening springs from a keen interest in plants and how we use them. My yard is a canvas; plants are my paint.

I think this is the result of being raised in the retail gardening trade. I recall a sign that was featured at our family stores that read, Weall and Cullen Nurseries. Where the Evergreen is KING! The sign was illustrated with a cartoonish spruce with a crown on its head. Dad had a sense of humour.

I find it interesting that the very place where that sign once hung at his store is now occupied by a bank. The currency of one business (evergreens) replaced the currency of another (cash).

Over fifty years later, here I am trading in words. I believe in the power of words. They can make peace and war, and what is more powerful than that? With respect to Winston Churchill's great wartime speeches, journalist Edward R. Murrow was widely quoted, "He mobilised the English language and sent it into battle."

Using words here, I reflect on the true meaning of what gardeners do. And the value of it. We are not launching war here or going into battle, just changing the world in a measurable and positive way, one plant at a time.

TRUE VALUE

In Washington, DC, at a subway station on a chilly winter morning, a man played a violin. Six pieces of Bach in forty-five minutes. About two thousand people walked by, most of them on their way to work. About four minutes into his performance the first dollar was dropped into his violin case. Ten minutes later, a small boy tugged at his mother's sleeve, encouraging her to slow down and take in the music. The mother pulled back hard, and they were on their way. This happened a few times during the performance: children trying to slow down their adult company to listen. Every time, the bigger person won the tussle and they moved on.

During the performance, six people stopped to listen for a short while and in total the violinist collected thirty-two dollars. As he packed up, no one noticed that he had stopped playing. No one applauded.

Two nights earlier the musician, Joshua Bell, had played to a sold-out crowd in Boston where the average seat sold for over one hundred dollars. He played on a violin valued at more than $3.5 million. Mr. Bell is acclaimed as one of the most talented classical musicians of our time.

The *Washington Post* had created this social experiment about perception, taste, and people's priorities: in a commonplace environment, at an inappropriate hour, do we perceive beauty?

My keenest sense of beauty during the gardening season is early in the morning, when the birds are singing, and the smell of fresh earth is rising. All my senses are on alert. I feel alive as I experience a symphony of sensations. I hold those images and feelings in my mind for times like this, when the snow is heavy on the ground and frost is on the windowpane.

The closest I come to that feeling this time of year is to listen to music like that of Joshua Bell. I close my eyes to imagine images of life in my garden as I know them in the growing season.

WHAT IS THE VALUE OF WHAT WE DO AS GARDENERS?

It is hard to say what the value of our work in the garden is. If you walk past a beautiful front yard garden in full bloom while on your way to work, chances are you won't see much. However, on a weekend morning on your way to the local playground with your three-year-old in hand, you may see it differently. Especially if your kid tugs at you and pulls you down to look at a butterfly on a flowering shrub. What do you see then? Through the filter of a pair of young, fresh eyes, you suddenly see the wonder of it all. You see hope.

To answer the question, "What is the value of a gardener's work?" we need to ask another question, "What is the value of nature?"

There was a time when gardeners saw themselves as warriors, determined to slay the aggression of the wilderness. We strived to take control. That is why gardeners just a couple of generations ago embraced the use of pesticides like 2,4-D, malathion, Cygon 2E, and Brush Killer D—the latter being the only product on the retail market that would kill poison ivy.

We still do our share of controlling. We cut the grass, trim the hedge, and hack back the aggressive growth of the evergreens in the yard. But there are great changes afoot in the Canadian garden.

We are planting record numbers of native plants. The word *biodiversity* has entered our lexicon. Many gardeners are making special efforts to attract hummingbirds, songbirds, bees,

and butterflies to create a more biologically diverse environment right in their own yards. We are conducting a social experiment of our own every time one of us signs up to produce food in a local community garden.

In the ever-changing world of gardening, where our work is never finished 'cause Mother Nature is forever changing it, I believe that there is more value in being a gardener today than at any time in our history. And I am very glad to be a plantsman.

Chapter 22

the Value of Urban Trees

*A seed hidden in the heart of an apple
is an orchard invisible.*

—Welsh proverb

The urban tree canopy plays an important and distinct role in Canada. While the country is home to 10 per cent of the world's tree canopy, our cities are starving for more trees. Tree count in every urban centre is in decline and has been for a couple of generations. This has a lot to do with disease like Dutch elm, the emerald ash borer, development intensification, and a general malaise about the whole affair.

If we are on the cusp of great change in Canadian horticulture (and I dearly hope that we are), planting and nurturing more urban trees must be at the top of our list.

I fear that we are doomed if this is not so. I hope that this story helps to shed light on the reasons why.

Next time you take a breath, be sure to thank a tree. The numbers are in and they are impressive. We can stop arguing over the importance of a healthy urban tree canopy, devote more time to celebrating heritage trees and planting and protecting urban trees. Based on new research, I believe that it is time to elevate the discussion.

URBAN TREE STUDIES

In 2014, TD Bank published a much-ballyhooed study on urban trees titled *Urban Forests: the Value of Trees in the City of Toronto* that deserves our attention. If you didn't get a chance to read it, let me summarize the salient points for you:

🌱 The City of Toronto urban forests are worth an estimated $7 billion, or $700 per (mature) tree.

🌱 For every dollar spent on tree maintenance, the urban forest returns $1.35–$3.20 worth of benefits and cost savings each year.

It may interest you that there are 116 tree and shrub species in the southern Ontario urban forest, in Toronto it covers nearly 30 per cent of the city (when viewed from the sky), and the average density of trees in the city is 16,000 per square kilometre, or four trees per person.

The TD study touches on important issues like air quality and water preservation, carbon storage, and property values (of interest to every property owner, I should think). I will return to this in a moment.

An expansive study in the United States is equally informing and impressive for its massive scale. In April 2015, the US Forest Service published the first ever national study in the *NRS Research Review* of the effects of trees on human health. No other scientific study has been quite this thorough. Here are some illuminating numbers (all US):

❧ 17.4 million tonnes of air pollution were removed by trees in the US annually, with the human health effects valued at $6.8 billion.

❧ Pollution removed from urban areas in one year equals $4.7 billion.

❧ Each year, 850 lives are saved, thanks to the environmental benefits of trees (mostly due to a reduction in respiratory disease).

❧ In one year, there are over 670,000 fewer acute respiratory symptoms among urban dwellers.

❧ In recent years, there have been 17 million trees removed from urban areas annually.

❧ According to the authors, "In terms of impacts on human health, trees in urban areas are substantially more important than rural trees due to their proximity to people." Scientists, I find, can sometimes be masters of stating the obvious. This is one weighty paper, with over eighty references to support it.

The point is this: *we need to learn to live with trees, and we need more of them.*

NATIONAL TREE DAY

Here in Canada, the third Wednesday of September is National Tree Day by act of Canadian Parliament.

What does that mean exactly? Well, it means that we really need to stop and think about what we are going to do to enhance our green urban environment. Perhaps the easiest thing for homeowners to do is to plant a tree. Find a place in your yard where a tree can serve a special purpose. Be selfish about it and think about the shade of a leaf-bearing tree (deciduous) on the west or south side of your home, cooling it and reducing the need for summertime air conditioning. An evergreen (coniferous) tree on the west or north side of your home will reduce the cooling impact of winter winds and save you heating costs. A large shrub that shades your air conditioner will save up to 15 per cent in air conditioning costs as well.

THINKING OUTSIDE THE BOX

A fruiting tree like an apple, pear, or cherry will provide you and your family with nutritious food in season. Many native trees provide fruit that attracts birds and other wildlife. A service-berry can be treated as a large shrub or trained as a tree (with annual pruning). It flowers early in the spring and is essentially insect- and disease-free. I love this native shrub tree for its versatility: it grows in sun or partial shade, in a wide variety of soil conditions, and songbirds forage for the berries. The serviceberry outside of my reading room window attracts cedar waxwings early each summer.

Not everyone reading this lives on real estate that provides the opportunity to plant trees. Consider joining the many volunteer organizations that are committed to enhancing the urban tree canopy. Your local municipality will be able to direct you to not-for-profit organizations in your community that could use your volunteer help planting trees.

TWO MILLION TREES FOR OUR HEROES

On Canada's official Highway of Heroes, which stretches from CFB Trenton to the coroner's office in Toronto, the Highway of Heroes Living Tribute is planting 117,000 trees, one for each of our war dead since 1812. Plus, we are planting 1.8 million more trees on the margins on either side of the highway, one for every Canadian who volunteered for military service during times of war.

I say "we" 'cause I am the volunteer chair of this campaign. We are raising $10 million to get the job done by 2022. If you like the idea of this project, why not consider donating to support it and plant a tree. Whether or not you have property of your own to plant trees, your "Hero" tree will be in good company, guaranteed. (See hohtribute.ca for details.)

MY OWN TREE PLANTING

Personally, I have enjoyed watching over two thousand trees grow on our four-hectare property since we moved here fourteen years ago. Almost nothing compares to the joy that I feel when I measure the progress each one of them has made in a short time.

Craig Alexander, chief economist at TD Bank Group, concludes their urban trees study with these words: "The cost of savings produced by our urban forests make it clear that keeping the green on our street, keeps the green in our wallets."

It is comforting to know that regardless of what motivates you, our commitment to a healthy tree canopy is one that we can take to the bank.

Come September, I wish you a Happy National Tree Day.

Part IV

Sowing
a Vision

I DREAM IN TREES.

Time was, I dreamed in colourful gardens. In 2006, I published a book called *A Sandbox of a Different Kind: 52 Short Gardening Stories*. In it I wrote a story about a dream where I was leaving for work, briefcase in hand (back when I carried a briefcase). It was mid-winter, but the leaves were on the trees and the garden was in full bloom. Remember, this was a dream. My wife, Mary, stopped me as the front door swung open to reveal this perfect picture. "It is much too nice a day for you to go to work. Why not stay home and work in the garden?" Which I did.

This dream is recurring, only these days I see trees and I hear birds—hummingbirds mostly, if it is a really good dream—rather than the broad sweep of impatiens outside my front door. You might not think that hummingbirds sing, but they do. With their wings. They hum. Like a bumblebee only louder. When they hover, they hum at a low pitch, when they take off, the pitch peaks as a helicopter does when the pilot pours on the gas.

Marsha Norman famously said, "Dreams are illustrations from the book your soul is writing about you." I suspect she was on to something there. I believe that all gardeners have an active dream life. It is a fringe benefit of being a gardener that we never talk about. We dream because we can. And not everyone can say that, at least, not to the extent that we can.

The experience of gardening stimulates us in unseen ways. Yesterday, at the end of the day, I came in to my home office and wrote my son Ben a long email that I had been composing in my head all day while in the garden. Normally I would not take on a creative writing project in the late afternoon, thoughts travelling more to the beer fridge than the computer. Yesterday was different. I had a story for Ben in my head that I had to write down before it was lost.

Perhaps I am unusual, but I write eulogies in my head while I am in the garden. I think of someone that I like and compose stories about them that are positive and fun. Think about it: when did you last attend a funeral where people didn't say the nicest things about the deceased? We never do that, not out loud, before they are gone.

Eulogies are composed of happy thoughts. While I write them in my head I often whistle or hum. As if being in a garden is not pleasant enough, eulogy writing and all the happy thoughts that they entail makes the experience even better. In the garden I am in eulogy heaven. (Ha! Pun not intended, but I like it.)

This section is about dreaming. We—and I say "we" 'cause son Ben makes his first and only solo contribution to this book in this part four; you can expect to hear much more from him in future work—pitch our thinking forward to the world that we imagine, one where gardening continues to play a role in our leisure time activities:

Where trees are planted by a man with a dream (think of Ken Jewitt).

Where climate change causes many of our gardening habits to change.

Where insect hotels outnumber backyard bird feeders.

Where bees and songbirds, pollinators of all kinds, and the larger web of nature interact. They make love, have babies, find habitat, and sometimes eat one another. All of this in our backyards, often while we sleep.

We sleep and we dream.

We dream and we plan.

We plan and a new world evolves and comes to life.

Will you forgive me for repeating this message one more time? This is the best time in our history to be a gardener in Canada.

Will you dream with us?

Chapter 23

Lessons My Garden *has* Taught Me

*I suppose the pleasure of country life lies really
in the eternally renewed evidences
of the determination to live.*

—Vita Sackville-West (1892–1962), *Country Notes*

This story is a reflection on how I have grown as a gardener through the experience of gardening. Writing it was a bit like trying to explain the feeling of becoming a new father to someone who is about to have the experience.

Sometimes words are not enough. You just have to live it.

My garden and I are celebrating our fifteenth anniversary. When I contemplated the concept of starting a large garden on my wife's family farm property, she said, "It is a field of soybeans.

Go nuts." The natural landscape is flat as a pancake and it was treeless, as farms often are. Until I got hold of it and planted several thousand trees and shrubs.

I get ahead of myself. The story of how my garden was born goes like this: One hot summer evening in 2004 I walked onto the property from the road, a broken hockey stick in one hand (this was going to be a Canadian garden after all) and a hammer in the other. I drove that piece of smooth hardwood into the ground at a spot that "felt right." Far enough from the road to insulate us from traffic noise and close enough that we would not feel we were part of a relocation program designed to sequester us from some evil.

I had carved off four hectares without giving it a lot of thought. Well, I can tell you that I have given it plenty of thought since then, including long moments when I question my sanity. I can tell you that an area the size of almost seven football fields represents a lot of weeds, grass cutting, veggie harvesting, and bugs.

It has also become a source of unanticipated joy and the source of many lessons. Here are some of them.

Relax the Urban Standards

I meet a lot of Canadian gardeners who move to the country and forget to leave their city-styled garden sensibilities behind. When you move onto a big property you must change your standards. Our almost half hectare of grass is not weed free, nor is it perfect. It is green most of the year and that works just fine for me. I fertilize it three times a year, and that helps me attain some modicum of decorum without harming the environment (they took the phosphates out of quality lawn fertilizers). Generally, a weekly cut is all that is needed.

Birds Are My Friends

I loved birds before; now I appreciate them at a new level. They sing their heads off from early April through mating season, they provide colour and entertainment, and (here is the big bonus) they eat a tonne of mosquitoes. Go swallows, go! I have thirty-eight nesting boxes for bluebirds, but no bluebirds. Instead, I am very successful at attracting tree swallows and house sparrows. I love them all and every one of the nesting boxes becomes a home for my darlings each spring.

A Sustainable Garden Is Less Work

I decided over thirty years ago that I would garden using organic methods when our first-born child entered this world. Adapting sustainable gardening methods in the country has proven to be easier than I had imagined. I share crops with bugs and manage the persistent ones using environmentally responsible products like diatomaceous earth for potato beetles; Green Earth Bordo mixture for tomatoes, apples, and pears; and powdered sulphur for powdery mildew. I spray less, worry less, and enjoy eating vegetables fresh from the garden without having to think about when I last sprayed them with something from my arsenal, Ðcause I don't have one. Nothing like a carrot pulled from the ground, wiped on the leg of my pants, and munched right on the spot.

Some Places Are Best Looked At, Not Fussed Over

I sowed three large meadows into my garden when we first moved. One of them I mow twice a season, another once a season, and the one nearest the road I don't mow at all. I only mow in response to my greatest enemy: Canada thistle. Otherwise, I would not mow any of them ever. (I have yet to figure out why I have trouble with Canada thistle in one field and not another.)

Sit A While

I have park benches, lounge chairs, and a Muskoka chair: last count there are twenty-two chairs and benches in my garden. And none of them will ever get worn out from overuse. However, I sit and contemplate the view more often now than ever before. The combination of the sky, garden, and water leave me breathless sometimes. Breathless in a good way. Now I can sit in the smallest of gardens without feeling the compunction to get up and pull a weed or deadhead the roses. In my "urban garden days" this was not so, such was my pursuit of perfection. Currently, I am a "relaxed gardener in training," and making progress.

Nature Gives Us Cues

I have spent a lot of time racking my brain, trying to figure out where a plant should go, what plant to choose in the first place, and whether I should move it after a few years. Slowly it is dawning on me that Mother Nature is cueing me to the best garden design ideas. All I must do is observe and listen. See the previous lesson.

Paths Should Lead Me Home

Break out the rendition of "Swing Low, Sweet Chariot." I learned the hard way that the paths (not chariots) in my garden are critical to its success. I hired a designer who showed me a simple grid that connects buildings, activity areas, and architectural features like a henhouse and woodshed. Inside the grid are the meandering paths that interconnect and take visitors on a journey of discovery. I walk each path every day in the gardening season. This way I learn a lot about what is changing, what needs attention, and sometimes what just needs to be sniffed or cut and brought indoors, into my space of "unreality."

You may be wondering why a "professional" gardener like me would need to hire a garden designer to design his own garden. The answer is that I sometimes can't see the forest for the trees. In other words, the greatest opportunities to create the garden of my dreams came from someone else, someone who understands gardening in large spaces and who understands my dream of a pollinator and wildlife garden. Much of what I have accomplished is a credit to him. (Gordon Hayward, by the way. If you want the name.)

Food Is Beautiful

Am I the only one who thinks that a garden filled with edible bounty is a thing of pure beauty? It is not that I love to cook; I don't. I love what a food garden represents. Sustenance for a hungry world and the miracle of nutrition from the most powerful combination on Earth: seed, soil, sunshine, and water. These are the things that make my back ache in the nicest possible way each planting season. And then again during harvest.

Embrace New Friends

We all need friends. I now have a lot of new ones to add to my repertoire. One is a duck. Clark. He makes me laugh out loud with his antics. He has a girlfriend now, a domestic duck that waddled down from our neighbour to the north. Lois. Lois and Clark are Super Ducks. If a coyote ever gets them, I will cry. I try not to think about it. Country living forced me to face the realities of nature. Not all ducks that have passed through my life in the last six years have been as lucky as these two. Sounds stupid, I know. (Footnote: Clark and Lois did pass on, and I did cry. I miss my quacky friend and his wife.)

Breathe Clean Air

If thistles are my enemy and ducks are my new friends, the air is what binds together everything in between. We take our fresh air for granted. Here in Canada we are blessed with an abundance of fresh air; even our cities provide fresher air than many other urban centres in other parts of the world. It is a relative thing not to be underappreciated.

Breathe deep. Observe the sky, especially at night. Let the plants attract birds, butterflies, and other pollinators. I try not to think of all the sex going on out there while I sleep. Some things are none of my business.

the Old Man and the Tree

He who plants a tree
Plants a hope.

—Lucy Larcom (1824–1893)

Sometimes I marvel at what one person can do. Just when I start to think, *How can I make an impact on climate change?* or, *I am only one person, what difference can I make?* along comes a person like Ken Jewett. I met Ken a couple of years ago, when he stepped up to the plate to help the Highway of Heroes Living Tribute. I have grown to appreciate his commitment and sincerity.

Take this story for what it is worth, and please note the last paragraph. We really should keep people like Ken in mind when we are debating the meaning of what it is to be a Canadian.

It was just a tree. Straightening his back and inspecting the hole that he had just dug, he was pleased. This would make a fine home for a maple. Not just any maple but a sugar maple. And not just any sugar maple but a sugar maple whose mother lived in the neighbourhood.

And so, it was not just a tree after all. It was a native arboreal tree whose leaves mirrored an image on our national flag. Ken Jewett was working on his farm in Brooklin, Ontario, while in his early twenties when the thought occurred to him, *I want to plant more native Canadian sugar maples. This will be my life.*

He had a lot of living to do before he would commit himself to the task. After working in the forestry business, at age forty he started his own company, Marsan Foods (they make chili for Tim Hortons, for instance). At sixty-five years old, he handed the reins of the family business over to his son Graeme and committed himself to the promotion, education, and planting of Canada's tree, the sugar maple (*Acer saccharum*).

MAPLE LEAVES FOREVER

Twenty years later, Ken Jewett is busy every day with his charity Maple Leaves Forever (MLF). "I started MLF in 2000 with the mandate and determination to encourage the planting of native Canadian maple trees. Like any new venture it took time and patience to settle into where we are today," he explains. "We started by creating awareness of the MLF program by providing thousands of native sugar maple seedlings at local municipal public tree planting days. Later, we started planting saplings, larger trees that had a much better chance of survival."

Ken was not the first to think that this was a clever idea. In the 1880s, the Ontario government encouraged farmers to transplant sugar maple seedlings along their laneways and road allowances that were harvested from their own woodlot. They received twenty-five cents for each seedling planted, roughly a day's wages back in the day. Today, many of those same trees can be seen as you travel the rural areas of Ontario.

With today's MLF, landowners who commit to plant at least ten trees on their property (maximum fifty) can obtain stock from a list of thirteen approved nurseries and receive a 25 per cent subsidy on the purchase of each tree. There is no restriction on size. Ken explains, "Once approved online, you place your order. When you have paid your invoice, send us a copy of it and we will send you a cheque for 25 per cent of the cost of the trees."

The system is simple and straightforward. Since its inception, MLF has donated over $2 million to the tree canopy by way of this program.

WHY NATIVE SPECIES?

While visiting a tree farm in Ontario several years ago, Ken learned that all the grower's stock was imported from Oregon. Ken remarks, "This led us to meetings with the City of Ottawa and the National Capital Commission. Most of their maples were coming from Oregon. This turned into a seven-year frustrating challenge. We placed a half-page ad in the *Ottawa Citizen* addressed to the Governor General, the CEO of the National Capital Commission, and the mayor of Ottawa." The NCC acquiesced on their position when "tree people" objected.

ONTARIO ENVIROTHON

MLF is a lead sponsor of Ontario Envirothon, which involves over ten thousand elementary school students. The kids are challenged to develop their own ideas and proposals to help make the province more green. Each summer a competition of the best ideas is hosted by a different city. Ontario Envirothon is organized by Forests Ontario.

HIGHWAY OF HEROES LIVING TRIBUTE

The Highway of Heroes Living Tribute is a campaign to plant a tree for each of Canada's war dead since 1812 on the highway right of way. The Highway of Heroes runs a distance of 170 kilometres and is the busiest stretch of highway in North America. Every Canadian lost during

the Afghan conflict was repatriated at CFB Trenton and driven by hearse down the highway to the coroner's office.

When the idea of reforesting the Highway of Heroes was first hatched, Ken called Tony DiGiovanni, the executive director of Landscape Ontario, and asked if the 117,000 trees being planted were native. "Why, yes Ken. And many of them will be maples." This was all that Ken needed to hear as he stepped to the plate to make a $25,000 commitment. That was several years ago, in the early days of the campaign. The MLF donation was a game changer for our new organization.

WHAT MAKES US CANADIAN

When Canadians open up the debate about what makes us truly Canadian, I hope that someone will raise their hand and remind us that there are precious few Ken Jewetts in this world. Our country is a better place for him and his work.

Chapter 25

Digging Deep

A garden is the most forgiving of mediums.
—Fran Sorin, *Digging Deep*

What can we learn from the gardening experience? I consider this question often.

When a psychologist turns her mind to the effects that gardening has on the human brain, new doors are opened. Opportunities I had never imagined present themselves. I am given permission to relax and absorb nature, rather than work frantically pulling weeds and spreading mulch. I see plants as my box of crayons. And above all, I realize why many years ago someone created the word *paradise* from the Persian word for garden.

Ha! The nearest thing to heaven is just outside my door.

John Pigott, a good friend of mine, likes to say, "When you pass the bread it comes back buttered." Gardening is like this.

While it looks like we are caretakers (and we often believe that we are), the fact is we receive as much as—and often more than—we give. This is just one lesson that I learned from Fran Sorin in her book titled *Digging Deep: Unearthing Your Creative Roots through Gardening*, published by Braided Worlds and from which all of her quotes that follow are taken. In *Digging Deep*, Sorin explores the experience of gardening on a variety of levels and provides her own insights based on a lifetime of planning, digging, planting, maintaining her own garden, and designing gardens for others. I don't believe that her experience is unique, but many of her observations are, as she shares an extraordinary gift for making important points gained through a life of gardening.

One of my earliest memories is that of pulling my thumb out of my mouth at about the age of three to express a thought, only to have my older sister finish my sentence for me. It was handy to have her stand there and do the work for me while I did something that I preferred to do (suck my thumb). Fran Sorin is like the older sister who opens your mind to words and thoughts that had not occurred to you before, even though both of you have enjoyed similar experiences in the garden.

Digging Deep is an intellectual approach to gardening, and it may not be for everyone. I must admit, as much as I love to drive my car I would not enjoy reading a similar tome about the creative process of auto mechanics. So, let me summarize the five important lessons that I learned from her excellent book.

1. Live in spite of fear.
There is this temptation to go about planting the garden with an eye to avoiding making mistakes. None of us like wasting time, money, or effort. We place the tall plants at the back of a flower bed and the short ones near the front and purchase the same old salmon-coloured geraniums for the pots at the front door every spring.

Sorin reminds us that gardening provides the opportunity to live creatively: "We are pushing towards new growth," as the psychologist Rollo May says, "*not without fear, but in spite of it.*"

I remind you that there are no failures in the garden, only composting opportunities. Sorin would add that the "mistakes" you make in your garden often provide the most joy at the end of the day. And if you aren't making mistakes, you are not being creative—my first *aha!* moment.

2. Your garden is an expression of you.

Sorin reminds us that every garden is as different as every gardener. Now this might seem obvious and a bit trite, but she expands on the idea of our uniqueness as expressed through our gardens by drawing attention to the earth, from which all great gardens spring.

It is here, beneath the soil, that the real magic occurs. Roots go down in search of microbes that assist in the ability of a plant to pull moisture and nutrients from the soil. "It is a wise and forgiving medium, this earth of ours."

Hmm. I never thought of it that way before.

3. To imagine is to see possibilities.

"Somehow life gives us the message loud and clear that imagination is a Sunday-afternoon luxury that we should put away as we mature." Or haul out with a box of paints and brushes when it is convenient for us. Sorin points out that most of us lose that childhood sense of wonder and adventure when we grow up. The rare individuals who retain these qualities are labelled as artistic, creative, and/or gifted.

But artists are not so different from any of us. We just choose not to let our artistic genie out of the bottle; we hesitate to let our creative juices flow. What makes the creative types different from the rest of us is that they refuse to push their natural creativity underground.

Imagination, Sorin reminds us, never dies. The good news is that you can unlock the door to your natural creative ability and "set it free" in the garden. This might start by taking your kids' crayons out of the box and sketching some images of the garden that you have in your head. Who knows what that might lead to?

Stimulating your creativity can allow a sense of wonder to emerge, which "is not something that you achieve, but rather something to awaken, moment by precious moment." She reminds us that Einstein once famously remarked, "Imagination is more important than knowledge." Who would argue?

4. The power of observation.

"Observing is simply the act of consciously attending to or making note of something," writes Sorin. If only it was that simple, my visits to the front porch in search of hummingbirds would produce a rich harvest of inspiration. Alas, sometimes a hummingbird is just a hummingbird.

However, the point is that "great poetry is created out of a heightened sense of awareness." And if we are going to be truly inspired as individuals, we must start somewhere. You don't have to be a poet to appreciate the depth of beauty that can be found in your garden. There are days when it is comforting to know that nature provides the most reliable of companions, as Sorin reminds us: "Come what may, the seasons change, the birds will migrate, snowflakes will fall, bulbs will bloom from the soil, the sun will rise and set. We can rely on all of this, even when everything around us seems uncertain."

Sorin aptly notes, "Being in nature—really being there, not just passing through—can provide us with a profound sense of peace and belonging." Looking through the lens of a powerful telescope and observing all the wonders of the universe, we are filled with awe. In the garden we experience just that, only in reverse: the wonders of life under our feet can fill us with awe, too.

5. Discover.

Sorin opens a chapter with, "Often the scariest question to answer can be, What do I want." She asks us to reflect on the idea of walking into a restaurant, being handed a menu and having no clue about what to order. None.

Life is full of menus and choices and decisions. As we explore questions about the kind of garden that we want (Herbs for the kitchen? Peonies like grandma used to grow? A tree for cooling shade or fruit?), we exercise those unseen muscles that help us make bigger, more important decisions about life. Our gardening experience helps us develop our own equilibrium and focus. Sorin encourages us not to censor ourselves here, to just have fun.

WE ARE ALL CONNECTED WITH NATURE

I have read a lot about people who have a heart attack or experience a coma and leave the world as we know it only to come back thanks to defibrillation or good luck. They describe their experience "on the other side" in a variety of ways. Sometimes it is an "incredible lightness of being," or there is a bright light shining out of the darkness: it is sunny, flowers are blooming, and birds are singing.

I have never heard of someone who visited the afterlife, however briefly, to be greeted by a computer monitor or desk covered in unfinished tasks. Invariably, there is some sense that they are entering a world dominated by nature.

And there is perhaps the greatest lesson of all in Sorin's *Digging Deep*. While there are people who connect with nature very well, Sorin made me realize that all of us have that connection, we just bury it under a lot of other stuff. The gardening experience assists those of us who want to access the box that contains our connections with nature. It is the motivation to reach in and pull out the real you and access the secret of life itself.

Chapter 26

a New Vision of Urban Development

*Of all the underlying forces working toward
emancipation of the city dweller, the most important
is the gradual reawakening of the primitive instincts of
the agrarian.*

—Frank Lloyd Wright (1867–1959)

In the past, a sign that you had "arrived" was to join a private golf course. The nearer to the city, the greater the prestige attached to membership. How many millennials do you know who are golfing? How many enjoy fresh, organic, local food? My point, exactly.

I predict that, in a generation or so, there will be privilege associated with locally grown food, a view of an urban farm from your kitchen window, and local access to community-based food.

Here is a new measure of prosperity.

✺

Indulge me for a moment and imagine a new residential development of quality homes surrounding an eighteen-hole, championship golf course. A well-designed community of semis, townhouses, and fully detached homes are knit together by winding, well-treed streets. Every garage has a golf cart in it and every golf cart has two large garden trugs in the back.

Say what? Okay, change that golf course to a farm. And not just any old farm, the latest urban farm, where half of the green space normally devoted to the golf course is a huge garden that produces food for the immediate community. Fresh greens and produce are sold to local green grocers and restaurants. During the growing season, people travel long distances to see this place. And local residents only travel a few blocks to pick up their groceries, fresh from the land.

The other half of the farm is carved into half-hectare plots for part-time urban farmers. These are co-op farms where the farmers share equipment and trade produce: "I am long on cucumbers. Can I trade you for some of your beans?" These same farmers make their living through CSA. Clients, like you, sign on for a season's worth of produce and, for a fixed monthly fee, receive a basket of food fresh from the land; whatever is ready for harvest is distributed to the subscribers. You can have it delivered for a small fee or come and pick it up in your golf cart.

A portion of the farm is partitioned into community gardens for local residents who want to grow their own food and share the experience of gardening with other people.

When you get up in the morning, rather than check for tee times on your computer, you go online and check what produce is available and fresh on the community farm that day. You will also check the calendar of events at the local barn/community centre where courses on gardening, harvesting, preserving, food freezing, and cooking are offered daily.

While this may sound like a pipe dream, it is anything but. Every one of the ideas that I have presented above already exists in one form or another.

BURLINGTON, VERMONT

The idea that cities can feed themselves is gaining traction more than ever. In Burlington, the capital of Vermont, more than 8 per cent of the food consumed by the residents is produced within city limits. Not bad for a city of almost 50,000 people!

According to Peter Ladner, author of *The Urban Food Revolution: Changing the Way We Feed Cities*, we are relearning how to farm and applying that knowledge in most interesting ways. As he puts it, we are learning "how to pick up what we dropped beside the road to globalization, and how to take it down another road that combines the best of ancient farming wisdom with modern technology."

I am fascinated by many of the concepts reviewed in this book. Many of them remind me of activities that can be found in Canadian cities right now. We just have not learned how to organize ourselves in such a way as to take full advantage of this knowledge. It is like having many pockets of wisdom and valuable activity without knitting them together in a more meaningful way.

FOOD IN URBAN GREEN SPACES

Take our green spaces, for example. City people value green spaces to picnic, walk, ride a bike, walk the dog, and gaze upon. There are wide tracts of land in our cities that are quite suitable for agriculture, but not for development. Why not leave the valley lands to the conservationists, the table land to thoughtful development, and the in-between real estate, like the hundred-year flood plain and hydro corridors, to urban farmers?

What if every resident in urban centres across the country had access to fresh, homegrown food that has not been strip-mined in California or some other foreign place? Why can't we walk into our backyard and "shake the hand that feeds" us, as Michael Pollan, author of foodie-manifesto *In Defense of Food: An Eater's Manifesto* is fond of saying? The hand of a local, urban farmer, that is.

Let's give condo owners, social housing residents, and all other residents in our cities equal access to locally grown, healthy food. Why not share it so that all can benefit? Would not all of us become more "wealthy" as a result?

If you are not inclined to grow your own food, would you appreciate access to local food that is literally in your backyard? Would you enjoy living in a house that backs on to "green space" where your food is growing, neighbours are gathering, children are playing in the apple orchard, and everyone is learning new skills in the art of growing plants and food preparation?

Could a neighbourhood become a full-time celebration of the very best things in life? Not just food, but social interaction, education, and fun: community building blocks that are the sweet elixir of a model city.

Experience tells us, according to Ladner, that local food reduces our dependency on oil. A Canadian study on "food miles" estimated that sourcing fifty-eight food items locally or regionally rather than globally could reduce greenhouse gas emissions by about fifty thousand tonnes annually. That is the equivalent of removing almost seventeen thousand vehicles from the road.

The new "urban farming community" as envisioned by Ladner gets people out of their cars, encourages social interaction, the consumption of better quality (and less processed) food, boosts local employment and provides, according to Ladner, "a feast of spinoff health, community-building, exercise, green space, community safety, recreational and educational benefits." I will add this key point: real estate values are enhanced when they are within proximity of urban farming establishments. (As long as odour issues associated with livestock are addressed. No one likes living next to a pig farm.)

In future, Canadians will measure the desirability of their living quarters by new standards. And locally produced food will factor into a significant part of the equation.

Chapter 27

to Think Like a Plant

MARK AND BEN CULLEN

Success consists of going from failure to failure
without loss of enthusiasm.

—Winston Churchill (1874–1965)

We live in a world that has forgotten how to fail.

When did you last celebrate a failure? I reflected on this during a trip to Southern Ireland with my good friend and fellow gardening enthusiast Denis Flanagan. While touring the great gardens of the Emerald Isle, I picked up a coaster for my beer glass with a picture and quote on it from Samuel Beckett: "Ever tried. Ever failed. No Matter. Try again. Fail again. Fail better."

His words reminded me of one of my favourite garden quotes, I just can't remember who first said it, though it goes something like this: "There are no failures in the garden. Just composting opportunities." Here, an elaboration on the theme.

❧

We get a lot of gardening questions. Most of them are specific references to a plant, bug, or design challenge. Just yesterday we were asked what those leafy perennial plants are. "You know the ones?" he said.

We looked at each other, "You mean hosta?" Bingo! We were right. It is an intuitive thing.

There is another question, the question behind all questions: "How can I succeed in the garden?"

The answer begins with more questions. Do you know someone who can fish, who goes out in a boat and always comes back with a catch? What do they have that the rest of us don't? The answer is simple: they have learned to think like a fish.

Want to become a successful gardener? Learn to think like a plant.

DEVELOP PLANT LANGUAGE

In high school, there was a select group of gifted kids who successfully learned how to communicate in French. Turns out neither of us were one of them. People who are multilingual tell us that there is a lot of work in it, until you hit the sweet spot: a point where the grammar, syntax, rhythm, and sound make sense. It is a big night when you have your first dream in another language. That night, you arrive.

Mark dreams in plants, mostly trees. Several years ago, he became obsessed with the idea of doubling the urban tree canopy. Then one day he dreamed of a meeting of all of the tree-hugging professionals he knew. He invited them to explore the question of what all of them could accomplish if they worked together toward the same goal: more tree planting. The result was the Highway of Heroes Living Tribute and the plan to plant almost 2 million trees on Canada's busiest highway.

Ben is young, but someday he may dream in plants, too.

Since giving up on impatiens (or quite possibly they gave up on Mark), he has also been dreaming about bees. And birds, like tree swallows.

We like all plants, but not all plants like us. Most vegetable plants cooperate in our almost half-hectare veggie garden. Peas don't like us. Even when we attempt to grow peas together, we can't grow them.

Years ago, we discovered the answer to poorly producing veggie crops: chickens. Throw your wayward lettuce and pea plants to some chickens, and they will thank you for it by producing the finest brown eggs.

The answer for overproduction is the same. Kale won't stop producing an abundance of leafy goodness for almost four months, July through October. They say that kale has all kinds of redemptive health qualities that put it up there with the gods of tasty food. Neither of us can stand the stuff. But, by feeding our chickens armloads every day, we get our kale reconstituted through the gut of a chicken, poached on a plate every morning. What a way to feel like royalty.

HOW DO YOU LEARN TO THINK LIKE A PLANT?

Easy. By failing. Who has a beautiful and productive garden without a rigorous process of failure? It happens so often in the garden that we forget what it really is.

We plant a few hundred annuals and veggies each year. Divisions of perennials are planted in the spring or fall, and shrubs and trees are moved around the yard like interior decorators move furniture. Often a plant dies. Its failure to put down a root and thrive is not a slight on us, the gardeners, though it can be a disappointment. It is just part of the process; the same way film is expected to fall on the cutting-room floor. Before digital, of course.

Following the advice of a landscape architect some ten years ago, five red oaks were planted within a couple of metres of the house "to cool down the wall in the bright sunshine." They slowly expired as their young roots found the alkaline, clay-based soil. Dead as doornails. The other trees that were planted at about the same time matured and now shade the south and west walls of the house. Mission accomplished; failure overcome.

HOW DO YOU KNOW YOU HAVE ARRIVED?

An experienced gardener can spot a thirsty hanging basket at forty metres.

Experience will tell you from three hundred metres when the Japanese beetle has invaded a linden tree. How? You will just know. A trained eye, one that has been conditioned by experience, is better than a book. Or higher education, when it comes to that.

When you have looked at enough healthy linden trees you will know when one isn't right. You will have learned to think like a linden. Through experience and your natural powers of observation, you will have arrived. And you will be thinking like a plant.

Chapter 28

"Certified"

*In wilderness I sense the miracle of life, and behind it
our scientific accomplishments fade to trivia.*

—Charles A. Lindbergh, *Life* magazine, December 22, 1967

When we think of our "community," we generally think of the people who live in it. Together, we make up our community. Beginning today, I would like to encourage you to expand your vision of community by including all the creatures that we share it with. As this story developed in my head—and my life—I began to see my own community as much more than a place where humans gather. I hope that it expands your world also.

I am not sure whether I am qualified to be "certified" or I am just "certifiable." Others will determine. In the meantime, I am determined to make my yard and garden as wildlife friendly as I can.

According to the National Audubon Society, it is not difficult to improve the status of your outdoor living space ecologically. All you do is take Audubon's Healthy Yard Pledge to do your best.

Taking the pledge costs nothing and if you break it, there are no environmental police who will come to your door in the wee hours to haul you away. You will just have to live with yourself and the conscience that you were born with.

Here is the pledge:

I pledge, to the best of my ability, to

❏ *reduce pesticide use*

❏ *conserve water*

❏ *protect water quality*

❏ *remove invasive, exotic species*

❏ *plant native species*

❏ *support birds and other wildlife on my property.*

That is it. If you are a resident of any province, other than Alberta, that has severely restricted the availability and use of house and garden pesticides, you can check off the first point. You will have trouble reducing the use of chemicals that you can't access, but let's not get hung up on semantics. The point is that you would reduce your use of chemicals if you could.

As for water, if you sawed off your downspout to divert the rainwater into your lawn and garden, you can check off the second bullet. If you have a garden pond, give yourself a star and check off the third bullet.

As for invasive plants, if you pull weeds diligently and have a general understanding of what is invasive and what is not, tick off the fourth bullet.

If you plant some Echinacea or a serviceberry, monarda, cat mint, lily of the valley, or any native plants in your garden, tick off the fifth bullet.

And finally, if you feed the birds, provide a place for them to drink and bathe, and (very importantly) if you keep your cat in the house during peak bird activity hours, you can tick off the sixth bullet.

There, that was not so difficult, was it? And now, hopefully, you realize that your activity on your own outdoor piece of real estate is substantial and makes a difference. You are on your way to a full awakening. Perhaps in a season or two you will build your own insect hotel (see chapter 13).

CANADIAN WILDLIFE FEDERATION

Taking a pledge and taking action are markedly different. Personally, I prefer the approach of the Canadian Wildlife Federation (CWF). They will reward you with a written acknowledgement of your good work, once you prove to them that you have done it. This is called the Backyard Habitat Certification Program, and I hope that you will consider it seriously. The CWF recognizes those who try to turn their backyards into wildlife habitats. The program is free and all you have to do is fill out a form, include some pictures and a simple sketch, proving that you support the concept of creating and maintaining biodiversity in your yard.

It does not matter whether you have just a small patio or an acreage; if you are welcoming wildlife into your outdoor space, you qualify. The idea is to encourage Canadians to make efforts to "meet the habitat needs of wildlife and allow individuals to have the property designated as wildlife friendly." This, according to their website, is what it is all about. The emphasis of the Certified Backyard Habitat Program is to raise awareness of the impact that we have on the wildlife community *at large*. It is important, for instance, to know that the birds, butterflies, and beneficial insects that you attract to your yard impact in a positive way on the wildlife activity in your neighbour's yard, on the park down the street, and for that matter, on the outdoor space in your community.

This program is the naturalist's version of "Community Watch." Only we're not looking out for the bad guys so much as we are encouraging the good guys to come home, enjoy a meal, and hang out for a bit. With luck, the salamanders, newts, and nuthatches will have babies in your flora, and when you think about it, what could be more exciting, really?

Speaking of communities, it is the intention of the CWF to take the information that people send to them as they apply for certification and create a database of national conservation efforts, while protecting your privacy as you wish.

HOW TO GET CERTIFIED

To apply for certification, go to the CWF website at cwf-fcf.org. Search "How to Garden with Wildlife in Mind" in the search bar. You'll then be able to download the form, find tips on how to make your application, and read about what you will receive in the mail in a few weeks, should your application be accepted. I am planning on making an application myself.

While visiting the CWF website, be sure to check out the helpful articles that they provide for free: how to build a bee bungalow (or side split, only kidding), gardener to gardener (if you want to talk with other like-minded gardeners), gardening 101, and how to adopt a turtle.

Clearly the CWF has created a wonderfully informative website that will be of use to gardeners with even the slightest interest in attracting wildlife and doing the "environmentally right" thing. The website has a section designed specifically for kids, too, with games, colouring pages, encyclopedia information for older kids, and a whole lot more. (Besides, what kid would not want to adopt a turtle after being able to read all about them?)

While you and I pull weeds, plant for colour, for shade, and to frame the perfect view using permanent plants in our own yard, it is easy to forget there are benefits that extend beyond what we originally intended when we had our first conversation with a garden designer. Especially when we leave plants alone, avoiding the old-fashioned autumn sanitizing that used to take place in Canadian gardens only a generation ago.

Likely, without even thinking about it, you have created a neighbourhood habitat for wildlife within your own neighbourhood. Perhaps it is time to sign up for certification. Welcome to the community!

Chapter 29

Climate Change *is* Real *for* Gardeners

Don't knock the weather;
nine-tenths of the people couldn't start a conversation
if it didn't change once in a while.

—Kin Hubbard (1868–1930)

After a recent winter that was notably mild, I was motivated to calm the nerves of many gardeners who were alarmed to find their flowering shrubs and spring bulbs popping blossoms ahead of schedule. With a nod to climate change, here is one take on previously unheard of changes in the garden.

It is early spring. Everywhere I go these days the questions keep coming: "What do I do about my flowering crabapple that is in bloom *in March*?" or, "What do I do about my bulbs that are coming up three weeks ahead of schedule?" and, "What do you think of these record-high temperatures?"

These are good questions and I will answer them below, but in the meantime I would like everyone to relax for a moment and reflect on the past ten years of our climate experience. (If you are old enough, you can reflect on the last twenty-five years or so.) Gardeners have an interesting litmus test of their own when it comes to climate. Venturous souls that we are, the temptation to plant species that are generally not accepted in our growing zone is something that we do on a regular basis. A rhododendron in the heart of Toronto, Ontario, a peach tree in Halifax, Nova Scotia, and overwintering a fig tree out of doors in the Okanogan Valley, British Columbia, are judged to be the ultimate tests of nerve in gardening circles.

More accurately, they *were* the ultimate test of nerve.

When I started in the business in Toronto, working for my dad, Len, at Weall and Cullen Nurseries in the late seventies, we carried two varieties of Japanese maple: Atro (*Atropurpureum*, the mother of all Japanese maples) and Bloodgood (*Acer palmatum*) the expensive but deeper red alternative. Both were marginally winter hardy in the greater Toronto market. Today, any self-respecting, full-service garden centre will carry no less than ten varieties. A wide selection is now available at your local retailer, as they are often grown on Canadian nursery farms. They are grown by professionals in response to the ever-growing demand for something different. Plants that were hard to get in the past are now mainstream.

The same can be said for redbud (*Cercis canadensis*), which was very hard to find some years ago, but is now available at most zone 5 area retailers, including Halifax, Nova Scotia; Moncton, New Brunswick; Barrie, Ontario; and Invermere, British Columbia, to name a few. Add to the list flowering dogwood, firethorn, purple smoke bush, laburnum (golden chain tree), butterfly bush (*buddleia*) and you get the idea.

Yes, we experienced an extremely mild winter in 2015, and if you can hearken back to the turn of the season before, our spring did arrive with shorts on (or was it a bikini?) in mid-March.

The previous May, I trapped a possum while attempting to catch a raccoon in my backyard. A rodent so ugly that it is cute. (I let it go, by the way.) Not many years ago, the possum was unheard of north of the Canadian/US border and now they are here in abundance. Neighbours well to the north can look forward to their arrival in a few years. Or next year.

NEW BUGS AND
LINGERING BIRDS

In the bug world, we now experience the joys of the Japanese beetle in our roses, a pest that I read about in American gardening magazines when I was cutting my teeth in the business but had no experience with. (You control them with pheromone traps.)

Alas, the robins may not be going very far each winter, the geese spend the season flying in circles rather than straight south, and the mockingbird in my back garden mocks me fifty-two weeks of the year, relieving me of a winter break. This is our new reality.

BE MINDFUL AND ADAPT

We can now plant extraordinary flowering plants that we once would not have dreamed of. As I look in my crystal ball and consider the trajectory of my thirty-five years of weather experience in the garden, I see camellias in my zone 5 future, florist azaleas rather than just the hardy ones that limit our choices of colour. I see French hybrid grapes, like the award winners they are growing in Niagara today. And who knows, in time, we may be doing as they are in Vancouver today—growing palm trees around gas stations!

But I also see increasing droughts forcing us to embrace water-wise gardening, and mounting defences as invasive species and insects invade our native forests and gardens.

There is good news and sad news in all of this. Without making light of climate change's harms, a longer gardening season will no doubt encourage us to spend more time in our gardens and out of doors in nature's world of green. It is important to use this time outdoors to be mindful of the changes happening around us, and to adapt.

BE GREEN

It is instructive to reflect on how we can add the colour green to our gardens, keeping in mind that there are several motifs on the theme of green.

Green is the colour of peacekeeping (along with blue). In garden design, it does just that by bringing together other, bolder colours, on a palette that flows and is harmonized by green. It contrasts with hot colours, such as red and yellow, and blends blues and greys.

How much green is enough in your garden? The more the better. Observe nature and she will show you the way. A meadow of wildflowers is mostly green, with punctuations of colours that change during the season. Green brings harmony.

Green is cooling and relaxing. Our bodies seem to know that oxygen is manufactured by the green living world around us. This is one reason why we are we drawn to the shade of a tree when looking for a place to spread the picnic blanket.

There are plants that give us reliable green, in various shades, too.

For dark green look for rhododendrons, peonies, Sarcoxie euonymus, and pachysandra.

For pure green, look for hellebores (and enjoy the early spring blossoms and deer-resistant foliage all summer), leafy shrubs like lilac and alpine currant, most shade trees and daylilies when they are not flowering, and of course ferns.

For grey/green, try *stachys*, dusty miller, silver mound *artemisia*, Japanese fern, blue fescue grass, hostas Elvis Lives and Blue Ivory.

For yellow green, I like August Moon and Gold Standard hostas, Japanese forest (and fountain) grass, moor grass, many yellow foliage evergreens like Old Gold juniper, golden threadleaf cypress, golden ninebark shrub, Emerald 'n' Gold euonymus, and Sunspot euonymus, and with trees you cannot beat Sunburst locust.

The answers to the first questions posed here are: don't worry about the early flowers on your crabapple or flowering almond, nor should you lose any sleep over the daffodils and tulips that are saying hello ahead of schedule. Don't worry, and be happy that you are not a fruit grower in this changing climate. Fruit tree growers live in fear that the blossoms on their trees today will be hit with hard frost tomorrow, thereby wiping out that year's crop.

Gardeners, on the other hand, could lose the flowers on hardy shrubs and trees prematurely, maybe some flowering bulbs in full bud will wilt if we get minus five or colder. In that sense, we are the lucky ones—all we really have at stake is pride, and the winter's long anticipation of a great show come spring. The same long winter that didn't come this year.

Chapter 30

Finding Meaning *at* the "End *of* Growth"

BEN CULLEN

The end of economic growth does not necessarily mean we've reached the end of qualitative improvements in human life.

—Richard Heinberg,
The End of Growth: Adapting to Our New Economic Reality

My son Ben recently joined me in the "business." He worked hard for his diploma in agriculture at the University of Guelph, then a business degree from Dalhousie University in Halifax, a few years in the corporate world of food, and then a unique education as he travelled in Europe, Russia, Mongolia, and in China on the Rusty Rooster, a rickety old train, by himself.

He comes to work with a new, younger person's perspective that is steeped in the thoroughly thoughtful mind of the person that he is and always has been. He is fortunate to have the intellect and insightfulness of his mother.

This is his single solo contribution to our book. And I love it. You will be hearing more from Ben in time. And his brief, though not insignificant, solo contribution to *Escape to Reality* marks the beginning of a gardener/thinker who will help lead a new generation to dirty knees and fingernails.

This is Ben Cullen, into the future.

ᵂ

For pretty much the entire course of human history we have taken for granted a notion of progress, which dictates that with every generation we get richer, wiser, and healthier than our forebears. It is sort of embedded in the human psyche that our pursuit in life is to outdo our parents and grandparents, and often we define this for ourselves in material terms: a bigger house, a nicer car, and better technology than our parents and grandparents could imagine in their lifetimes.

It is a behaviour that is finally coming up against its limits. As it was famously put by peace activist, poet, philosopher and (ironically) economist Kenneth Ewart Boulding, "Anyone who believes in indefinite growth in anything physical, on a physically finite planet, is either mad or an economist." Indeed, we are nearing the end of a very long growth spurt.

In *The End of Growth: Adapting to Our New Economic Reality*, Richard Heinberg makes a compelling argument that resource depletion, environmental degradation, and "crushing levels of debt" have basically eliminated the possibility that the twenty-first century will be as materially prosperous as the twentieth century was for the majority of North Americans, and the social strains are already revealing themselves.

Generation Squeeze is a lobby group representing the interests of Canadians and, as they put it, "Canadians in their twenties, thirties, and forties today are working and studying more to have less." The topline numbers are indeed staggering: inflation-adjusted earnings are down an average of 11 per cent for a generation that is more than twice as likely to have post-secondary education, and an average home costs $490,000 compared to the $210,000 that our parents expected to pay. If you were wondering where the brooding millennial stereotype comes from, there's your first clue!

But feelings of discontent are misplaced. While many of us are feeling shortchanged on a dream that was sold to us, there is an emerging wisdom among millennials who are turning their backs on the rampant consumer pursuit. For example, for the first time since the advent of the automobile, studies show that young people no longer view cars as a status symbol. When entering the real estate market, young people are increasingly moving toward smaller dwellings in dense neighbourhoods where there is easy access to our communities. Mercifully, my peers do not consider me a failure for the fifteen-year-old Toyota that I get around in, or the rental apartment where I sleep, a ten-minute walk from the centre of town. This contrasts with the black-and-white photograph of Grandma and Grandpa at my age, smiling next to the new Chevy parked by a newly built detached home of a postwar subdivision. I think many families have a version of this photograph filed somewhere in their family archives.

Grandma and Grandpa were able to point at the new Chevy as a 1.5-tonne steel and chrome monument to how far they had come, a massive leap from the desperate conditions of their Depression-era upbringing. That was indeed progress, a generation which leapt so far that they could coin the term "standard of living," and cars were an important symbol.

But for the material testament to this leap, how much contributed to "quality of life"? Quality of life has always been a product of health care, education, arts, freedom of movement, and access to quality food. These are the things that make life *better*, and if you've ever tasted a liver sandwich or opened an old textbook, you would know that we continue to make tremendous progress in these areas. Cars and houses have only ever been a way to get around and a place to sleep, but they do serve as important symbols.

What symbols will our generation choose to define our progress? It helps to look at areas where there is still lots of work to be done. Our environmental deficit comes to mind, and access to quality food is improving, but there is still plenty of work to be done. There is a historic opportunity for our generation to be defined by the "material" improvements we can make to these monumental problems.

There is great satisfaction in taking control of matters with your own hands. Start by finding out about opportunities to participate in environmental healing—tree plantings, demonstrations (of skills and of political rancour), or planting and rejuvenating in public and private spaces. If you don't have a space of your own, look up community gardens in your area where you can till your own row. Share your surplus harvests to improve food access in your community, and when your garden is at its peak in mid-July, smile for the photograph.

ACKNOWLEDGEMENTS

Anybody who has written a book knows that it does not happen overnight and that the author—two of us in our case—is not entirely responsible for the content. It takes, as they say, a village. In our case, a village of heavy lifters.

First, we wish to thank Jane Van Der Voort, our editor at the *Toronto Star*. It is our goal in life to meet her standards for journalistic excellence. Jane is the second toughest editor that Mark has worked with in his long writing career (this is his twenty-third book). This is a compliment to Jane. What would otherwise be an old pair of boots is clean, shiny, and proud. Jane makes our work so.

To Brenda Hensley, our assistant. Like a dog on a bone, a husky (her favourite) to be precise, Brenda researches facts, clarifies otherwise fuzzy ideas, and reminds us of deadlines. Brenda is our master and commander who walks softly and carries a feather duster, on a big stick.

To mom and wife, Mary Cullen. Ah yes, our number one cheerleader and best supporting actor. Except that she can't act as that would require not being herself, which she specializes in. Truth is, Mary is an inspiration and the whole reason why Ben and Mark are a team. 'Nuf said. We love her.

To Paula Sarson, our editor at Nimbus Publishing. Such an easy to get along with editor. And yet, precise, grammatically correct, and a master of sentence structure. Paula makes the English language flow easily.

Also at Nimbus Publishing, the team has been magnificent. Whitney Moran, Karen McMullin, and Terrilee Bulger among many are keeping the literary lights on in the Canadian

Maritimes and abroad. Theirs is a mission that we are proud to be a part of. Thank you for believing in us, ever so much.

Thank you to Jenn Embree, who designed the book's beautiful interior and, along with art director Heather Bryan, the cover. And to artist Sarah Duggan, who provided lovely original artwork to complement the essays.

And finally Mark wishes to thank Ben, for opening his mind to a world of gardening through the eyes of youth.

To all of the "under 40s" who have picked up the trowel, who get their knees dirty: you inspire us all and give us hope.

Mark and Ben Cullen

Selected Bibliography

Ellis, Hattie. *Sweetness and Light*. New York: Three Rivers Press, 2004.

Heinberg, Richard. *The End of Growth: Adapting to Our New Economic Reality*. Gabriola Island, BC: New Society Publishers, 2011.

Jacobsen, Rowan. *Fruitless Fall*. New York: Bloomsbury, 2008.

Johnson, Lorraine. *The Gardener's Manifesto*, Toronto: Penguin Canada, 2002.

Ladner, Peter. *The Urban Food Revolution: Changing the Way We Feed Cities*. Gabriola Island, BC: New Society Publishers, 2011.

Northern Research Station (NRS), U.S. Forest Service. "Trees Improve Health and Well-Being in Many Ways." *NRS Research Review* 26 (April 2015): 1–7.

Packer, L., J. Genaro, and C. Sheffield, "The Bee Genera of Eastern Canada," *Canadian Journal of Arthropod Identification* no. 3 (September 25, 2007), doi: 10.3752/cjai.2007.03.

Packer, Laurence. *Keeping the Bees*. Toronto: HarperCollins, 2010

Pollan, Michael. *In Defense of Food: An Eater's Manifesto*. Penguin Group, 2008.

Saul, Nick, and Andrea Curtis. *The STOP: How the Fight for Good Food Transformed a Community and Inspired a Movement*. Toronto: Vintage Canada, 2014.

Sorin, Fran. *Digging Deep: Unearthing Your Creative Roots through Gardening*. Philadelphia, PA: Braided Worlds, 2016.

TD Economics. *Urban Forests: the Value of Trees in the City of Toronto*. June 9, 2014, www.td.com/document/PDF/economics/special/UrbanForests.pdf.

Wulf, Andrea. *The Invention of Nature: Alexander Von Humboldt's New World*. New York: Alfred A. Knopf, 2015.

WEBSITES

Bees Are for Life: beesarelife.ca

Canadian Wildlife Federation: cwf-fcf.org

Community Food Centre: cfccanada.ca

Composting Council of Canada: compost.org

Cultivate Toront: cultivatetoronto.com/landsharer

Food Share: foodshare.net

Forests Ontario: forestsontario.ca

Free-Range Kids: freerangekids.com

Fresh City Farms: freshcityfarms.com

Highway of Heroes: hohtribute.ca

Maple Leaves Forever: mapleleavesforever.com

Mark Cullen: markcullen.com

Plant a Row, Grow a Row: growarow.org

The Stop: thestop.org

Wychwood Barns: artscapewychwoodbarns.ca

Young Urban Farmers: youngurbanfarmers.com

Mark Cullen is the president of Mark's Choice Ltd., the spokesperson and horticultural consultant to Home Hardware Canada, spokesperson for Premiertech Home and Garden, Member, Order of Canada, and a volunteer spokesperson for SHARE Agricultural Foundation, Canada Blooms, and founding chair of Highway of Heroes Living Tribute. As a garden communicator, Mark reaches over 2 million Canadians every week. A bestselling author of over 500,000 books in Canada, Mark has written over 20 books, including his most recent, *The New Canadian Garden*. Visit markcullen.com.

Officially, **Ben Cullen** joined Mark full time in 2017. Unofficially, Ben has worked with Mark his entire life. Ben's interest in growing really began while working at the local golf course through high school, before heading off to complete a Diploma in Agriculture at the University of Guelph. Afterwards, Ben headed east where a Bachelor of Commerce from Dalhousie University in Halifax led him into the food industry. Recent travels have taken him overland from London, UK, to Shanghai, China. Since returning home he has enjoyed channelling his passion for food, travel, and growing back into Mark's original mission—connecting and inspiring people with things that grow.

CANADIAN SOLDIERS LIVE FOREVER

Join us in planting two million trees along the 401 Highway of Heroes, a tribute to the men and women who fought for Canada in our wars, and a living memorial to the 117,000 who died for freedom.

You can participate in honouring our military, protecting the environment and beautifying North America's most travelled highway. Visit **hohtribute.ca** or call **(905) 875-0021** and get involved.

Campaign Cabinet: Mark Cullen, Donna Cansfield, Michael de Pencier, Tony DiGiovanni, Trish Long, Valerie Pringle and Elaine Solway